Frank Hurley in Papua

Frank Hurley in Papua

Photographs of the 1920-1923 Expeditions

Jim Specht and John Fields

Robert Brown and Associates in association with the Australian Museum Trust

THIS BOOK HAS BEEN PUBLISHED IN ASSOCIATION
WITH THE AUSTRALIAN MUSEUM TRUST TO COMMEMORATE
THE CENTENARY YEAR OF THE COLONIAL ANNEXATION
OF PAPUA NEW GUINEA.

Designed and published by
Robert Brown and Associates (Aust) Pty. Ltd.
P.O. Box 29
Bathurst, N.S.W. 2795 Australia
First published 1984
Copyright © Australian Museum Trust 1984
Distributed in PNG by
Gordon & Gotch (PNG) Pty. Ltd.
P.O. Box 107
Boroko, P.N.G.
Printed in Singapore by Toppan Printing Co

National Library of Australia
Cataloguing-in-Publication data

Specht, Jim, 1940-
Frank Hurley in Papua

Bibliography
ISBN 0 909197 90 3

1. Photography, Documentary. 2. Papua New Guinea —
Social life and customs — Pictorial works.
3. Hurley, Frank, 1885-1962. 4. Photographers —
Australia — Biography. I. Fields, John, 1938-
II. Hurley, Frank, 1885-1962. III. Australian Museum.
IV. Title.

779'.99953

All rights reserved. No part of this publication may be
reproduced, stored in a retrieval system, or transmitted in any
form or by any means, electronic, mechanical,
photocopying, recording, or otherwise, without the prior
permission of the publisher.

Contents

Foreword	1
Map	2
Introduction	3
Photographs	11
Port Moresby	12
South-east Coast	32
North Coast	52
Central Province	78
Lake Murray	100
Fly River Delta	112
Aramia River	124
Papuan Gulf	140
Bibliography	193

Acknowledgements

A book such as this could not be prepared without considerable assistance from librarians and permission from the copyright holders. We express our sincere thanks to the staff of the National Library of Australia in Canberra for assisting us in the viewing of the Hurley negatives, manuscripts and newspaper cuttings held by the Library. We are indebted to Mrs A. Mooy (Toni Hurley) for her willingness to allow us to quote freely from her father's diaries, without which the commentaries would have been impossible. Permission to quote from *The Sun* newspaper was granted by John Fairfax and Sons Ltd, Sydney. We also wish to thank the Director and Trustees of the Australian Museum for their permission to embark on this project in the first place.

June Adams began the unenviable task of typing our manuscript, but the main burden of this was carried by Florence Burns. To Florence we extend a special word of thanks. Tracy Ryan made many useful comments on matters of style and proof-reading. Tony and Jenny Crawford gave us encouragement as well as friendship and hospitality. Darby Price, a former associate of Frank Hurley, has worked voluntarily at the Museum for some years and through this assistance has greatly facilitated our task in many ways, particularly in helping to conserve the fragile glass negatives. A special word of thanks must go to Howard Hughes, formerly head of the Museum's Photography Department, who recognised at an early date the significance of the negatives and ensured their conservation and transfer to film negatives. His personal collection of newspaper clippings by and about Hurley has proved a most useful source of information.

J.R.S. & J.J.F.

Foreword

In the eyes of Europeans and most Australians at the turn of the century, New Guinea was an island of mystery inhabited by strange and primitive people. The cultural differences between the colonisers and the colonised were so great that neither side could understand and appreciate the other; both sides interpreted the situation in terms of their own cultural backgrounds. The Germans, British and Australians recorded their attitudes and reactions in a wide range of documents and publications, but the indigenous response is almost totally unrecorded. Today, one hundred years after colonial annexation, much of that information has been lost with the passing of generations, and that period of Papua New Guinea's history will be known almost exclusively from the outsider's point of view.

A partial remedy for this dilemma may be sought in the study of photographs taken by the early colonists and other visitors. For Papua, the photographs taken by Captain Frank Hurley in the 1920's are a major starting point for understanding that period. These photographs, acquired by the Australian Museum Trust in 1927, are both a portrait of Papuan cultures and a statement on the colonial situation of 1921-23, as well as a reflection on the ambitions and expertise of Hurley himself. But, like all historical documents, their interpretation is not an easy, or obvious, exercise. Irrespective of whether the viewers are Papua New Guinea nationals trying to understand their own past or people from other cultures, we must be aware that we tend to project our own ideological preferences and prejudices into our interpretations of the past. This filtering of perspectives on the past through personal experience and present attitudes increases as we move back in time and rely on non-literary forms of evidence. Realisation of this should not deter us, however, from offering our interpretations, but should encourage us to make known the ideological basis on which our interpretations are developed. This volume of Hurley's photographs is not a history of colonial Papua in 1921-23; that must await a very different kind of book. Here we have a book which draws attention to the existence of these important historical records and to an important phase in Hurley's long and distinguished photographic career.

This selection of photographs represents less than 10 per cent of the Hurley collection held by the Australian Museum. Some have been published previously, but many are presented here for the first time in print. They are not all masterpieces of photography; some are decidedly below Hurley's technical best, but are included for the commentary they provide on Hurley himself, the situations depicted, or the difficult circumstances under which he was often working.

As historical documents, the photographs are multi-facetted, but they are first and foremost Hurley's descriptions of lifestyles now largely overtaken by cultural change. They show details rarely captured in academic or other writings. Hurley himself noted in one of his diary entries that words were inadequate to describe the scene inside a longhouse on the Fly River delta. The photograph not only conveys more information but places it in a context: where people sat, how tools and utensils were stored, what food was prepared and eaten, and so forth. This contextual information is frequently omitted from museum displays of other cultures, as well as from writings of the period. All too often these cultures are portrayed somewhat clinically as a series of artefacts displayed as disjointed elements of some systemic whole. Museums have been challenged justifiably by the Third World and by indigenous minorities to re-evaluate their portrayals of other cultures, particularly to express the insiders' perspectives of their own cultures. Museums have a major responsibility in this area and many, my own included, have sought in recent years to achieve a more integrated presentation of other peoples' cultures and the heritage of humankind. We still have a long way to go but, as with the problems of historical interpretation, at least the problem has been identified and a start has been made. Photographs such as these taken by Frank Hurley may provide clues for achieving those objectives.

The last decade has seen much concern throughout the world for the return of artefacts to their countries of origin, but accessibility to information about their cultural heritage through media such as photographs has received very little attention. I believe it is important in this year marking the centenary of colonial annexation of Papua New Guinea to emphasise the wealth of historical and cultural information contained not only in the Hurley photographs but in other collections held in public and private ownership around the world. Notwithstanding the points I have made above, these often constitute statements about the cultural heritage of no less importance than the artefacts.

I hope this presentation of Hurley's perspectives and interpretations of his time may contribute to a better understanding of the past of Papua New Guinea, and to a richer appreciation of the present.

D.J.G. Griffin,
Director,
Australian Museum, Sydney.

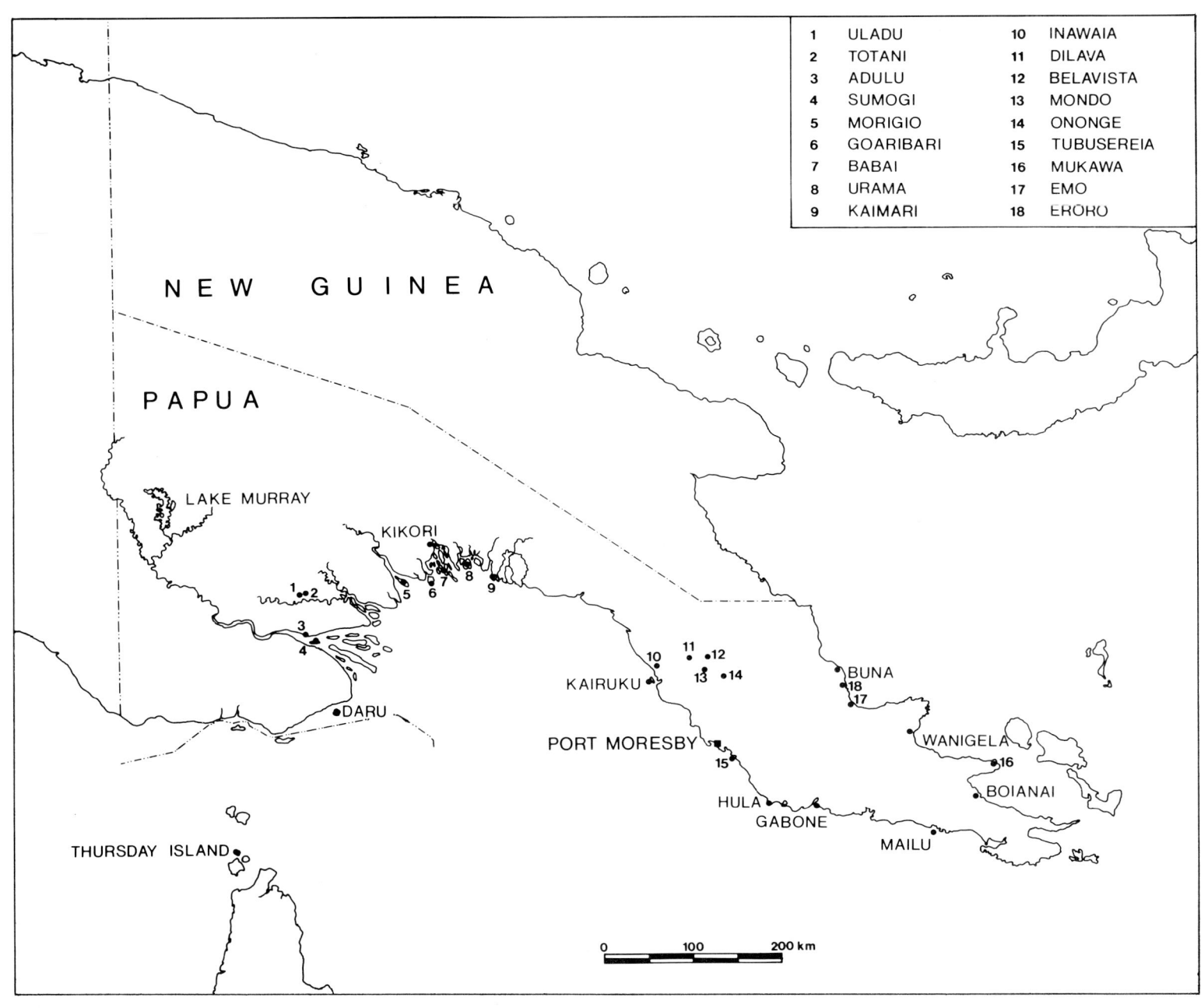

Map of Papua New Guinea, showing the main places visited by Frank Hurley during his two visits. The routes followed were:

1920-21: Thursday Island — Daru — Kairuku — Port Moresby — Gabone — Mailu — Emo — Wanigela — Mukawa — Boianai — Mailu — Hula — Port Moresby — Kikori — Urama — Kaimari — Kairuku — Dilava — Belavista — Mondo — Ononge — Inawaia — Port Moresby.

1922-23: Port Moresby — Kaimari — Daru — Thursday Island — Daru — Lake Murray — Adulu — Sumogi — Morigio — Uladu — Totani — Morigio — Goaribari — Babai — Urama — Kaimari — Port Moresby.

Introduction

In a photographic career spanning nearly sixty years, Frank Hurley secured for himself an international reputation for imaginative and innovative work. For many people today he is best remembered for some of his early picture postcard photographs, his First World War scenes or his documentation of Antarctic exploration. Few beyond a small coterie of anthropologists and archaeologists are familiar with his photographs taken in Torres Strait and Papua between 1920 and 1923. In presenting this small selection from the collection held by the Australian Museum, we hope to redress this situation and to draw attention to an important period in his career.

James Francis Hurley (1885-1962) was a man of great self-confidence, determination and ability. These qualities were displayed early in his life when he abruptly terminated his schooling in 1898, and ran away from his home in the Sydney suburb of Glebe to find work in a Lithgow factory (Bickel 1980). By 1903 he was back in Sydney and had bought his first camera. In the following year he obtained his first professional assignment for an advertising photograph for the American Edison Phonograph Company. With his father's financial assistance in 1905 he secured a partnership in the picture postcard business with Henry Cave. He soon established himself as a photographer of ability, with a flair for the unusual and the dramatic.

A turning point in his career came in 1911 when Douglas Mawson selected Hurley as the photographer for his first Antarctic expedition, during which he had responsibility for both still and movie photography. After more than a year in the Antarctic, Hurley recuperated in 1913 by taking a voyage to Indonesia, briefly visiting the then Australian colony of Papua.

His performance on Mawson's expedition led to an invitation to join Shackleton's Antarctic expedition of 1914-16. The expedition was a near disaster for Shackleton's party. His ship, the *Endurance,* was crushed by ice (an episode vividly recorded by Hurley) and the party became marooned. By sledging, floating on ice-flows and sailing in open boats, the party reached Elephant Island, over 1000 kilometres from the nearest source of help on South Georgia Island. While Shackleton took a small group to South Georgia to organise a rescue attempt, Hurley and the remainder of the party spent five months living under two up-turned boats through their second Antarctic winter. Hurley, an inveterate diarist, recorded that they discussed in addition to good food, warm baths and other home comforts, plans for holidays and other ventures in tropical places. The rescue was successful and he arrived in England in November 1916. There he began work on processing his photographs and editing the film, as well as meeting with other Antarctic veterans.

The results of the movie film were disappointing. When Shackleton's party had abandoned the crushed *Endurance,* most of the photographic materials were discarded, along with anything else not essential for survival. Hurley was dissatisfied with the surviving film footage and decided that additional material, particularly of wildlife, was essential. In February 1917 he sailed again to South Georgia to obtain these film sequences. Soon after his return to England, and before he had time to complete the film, he found himself recruited as an official war photographer, with the honorary rank of Captain, to record aspects of the Australian contribution in Europe and the Middle East.

Hurley married in 1918 and returned to Australia where he completed the Shackleton film. A settled family life in Sydney was interrupted in 1919 by the birth of twin daughters and by Hurley joining Ross and Keith Smith in Queensland to take aerial photographs on the last leg of their flight from England to Australia. The settled life was further interrupted in 1920 when he began the first of two extended visits to Torres Strait and Papua. This first expedition, lasting nearly nine months, was his first major independent venture for many years. Much of the time was spent at or around European settlements and in areas where cultural change was already well under way. Only towards the end of the expedition was he able to visit areas less influenced by government, missions and plantations. On his return to Sydney in August 1921 he prepared the initial version of his film *Pearls and Savages*. He felt the film was too tame, lacking in exciting and dramatic scenes, and promptly began planning for a return visit to improve the film and extend its scope.

Whereas the first expedition to Papua was a solo affair, the second was a team effort and better equipped. The team arrived in Port Moresby in two parties in August and September 1922. The expedition was arguably only a limited success, being fraught with unexpected difficulties of personnel, equipment and relations with the Papuan administration. But for Hurley, ever the optimist, it provided him with the spectacular film footage he needed to improve *Pearls and Savages*.

Hurley returned to Sydney in February 1923. In 1924 he personally promoted the revised film in the United States of America and Great Britain, and a book of the same title was published. In London the film's British premiere was held at Covent Garden on 31 October 1924. An instant success, it was heavily promoted by Stoll Films and ran for three months, three times daily, with commentary by Hurley himself, at the Polytechnic Cinema Theatre in Regent Street. The book was equally well received, going through three printings in nine months; a German translation and a Braille version were also produced.

These successes stimulated Hurley's interest in the developing feature film business, and he produced two films derived from his Torres Strait and Papuan experiences: *Hounds of the Deep,* and *The Jungle Woman.* The latter, very much in the idiom of the day, was originally planned for shooting in Papua. But Hurley's altercation with the administration in 1923 led Hubert Murray, as Lieutenant-Governor of the colony, to set such rigid and restrictive conditions that the film could not be made there. He was not deterred; he selected a new location in Irian Jaya, then under Dutch colonial administration. Neither film was especially successful, and they seem to mark the end of his involvement with the island of New Guinea. In 1927 he sold most of his Papuan and Torres Strait glass negatives to the Australian Museum, stating that "I have no further use for my extensive collection of Papuan Negatives and am disposing of them" (Australian Museum Archives 389/27: Hurley to Anderson, 8 March 1927).

THE FIRST EXPEDITION OF 1920-1921

Virtually nothing is known of Hurley's first visit to Papua in 1913; it is known only from references in later diaries to the changes which had taken place in Port Moresby between 1913 and 1921. The visit was apparently brief, merely a port of call while en route to Indonesia, and Hurley does not appear to have taken any photographs. His second visit lasted nearly five months, from 27 March to 19 August 1921, after his extensive tour of Torres Strait. The photographic 'catch' from both areas was over 1,200 glass negatives and 22,000 feet of movie film (Diary D, 27 August 1921).

While the first visit to the tropics in 1913 may have been to escape from the cold of the Antarctic, the 1920-21 expedition had very definite objectives: "my primary purpose is to take cinematograph films and plates for a travelogue entertainment" (Diary A, 2 December 1920). This 'entertainment' would be presented by Hurley in Australasia and by Lowell Thomas elsewhere, an arrangement which would enhance Hurley's international reputation. To facilitate the work, he arranged with the Australian Board of Missions to visit their stations and record them photographically for publicity purposes. In return, he would receive free hospitality at the stations and free local transport.

Lowell Thomas wanted to join him in Papua, but Hurley cabled from Port Moresby on 4 April 1921, telling him not to come. He could not afford to wait the several weeks, possibly months, it would take Lowell Thomas to reach Port Moresby. Moreover, Hurley found Port Moresby a town for which he could express only sentiments of distaste, both for its white population and its buildings. He was probably concerned, also, that too close an association with such an internationally renowned traveller as Lowell Thomas might lessen the recognition that he himself might receive from any film or travelogue that resulted from their collaboration. There are frequent references in the diaries of both expeditions to Hurley's sense of mission and challenge: ". . . .success is entirely within my own making" (Diary A, 5 December 1920); "I am out to make a hit and win success and realise that I can only secure it by my own efforts" (Diary B, 4 April 1921).

Hurley departed Sydney in early December 1920 and spent the first three months among the islands of Torres Strait, with two "cinematographs" (one for underwater filming), two still cameras, and a phonograph. He was disappointed with the Torres Strait islanders and islands. Thursday Island was "A collection of galvanised iron shanties hideous and ugly . . . .", while the mixture of peoples — Malay, Chinese, Japanese and islanders — was ". . . .a satire on the White Australia Policy" (Diary A, 13 December 1920). While he found worthwhile photographic subjects in the pearling and bêche-de-mer fishing industries, the islanders themselves were so thoroughly missionised that he despaired of obtaining good photographs of traditional life.

Leaving the Torres Strait islands on the *Tambar,* Hurley entered Papua via Daru. There the ship took on board 100 men from the Bamu River area for work in mines near Port Moresby, and Leo Austen, a government officer just returning from a patrol up the Fly River to investigate the murder of two prospectors, Drechsler and Bell. Hurley and Austen travelled together on the *Tambar* to Port Moresby, via Orokolo and Kairuku Island. Arriving in Port Moresby on 1 April 1921, Hurley found that the Lieutenant-Governor, J.H.P. (Hubert) Murray, was due to return from leave the following day. In the meantime, he made arrangements with Judge Herbert, serving as Murray's surrogate, for his tour of the mission stations. He also contacted Dr W.M. Strong, Government Anthropologist, for advice "in classifying native types etc.".

After delivering the Bamu River labourers and various goods to the Laloki mine near Port Moresby, the *Tambar* continued eastwards to Samarai, calling at several plantations and missions on the way. Among the passengers were Reverend and Mrs W.J.V. Saville from Mailu Island, where Saville was in charge of the London Missionary Society station. The Savilles invited Hurley to stay with them when his work on the north coast was completed. At Samarai he found the Anglican launch, the *Whitkirk,* waiting to take him to the north coast stations. The *Whitkirk* was placed at his disposal for eight weeks, though some of this time was spent on mission activities. This tour included all government and mission stations on the north coast, with only one trip any distance inland. Hurley returned to Samarai and took the *Tambar* to Mailu to join the Savilles. The last stretch back to Port Moresby was completed in the Saville's mission launch.

In Port Moresby the administration officials were cooperative and helpful. Murray placed the government vessel *Minnetonka* at Hurley's disposal for visiting the Kikori-Purari delta area in the Gulf of Papua. Previous conversations with Murray and other government officers and missionaries had whetted Hurley's interest in visiting the area and villages inland from Hall Sound near Kairuku Island. He proceeded to Kikori and joined the Assistant Resident Magistrate, R.A. Woodward, on brief visits to Urama Island and Kaimari village in the Purari delta area. These villages presented cultures which had experienced much less change than those he had previously visited. As a bonus, their spectacular large men's houses and mask forms provided the kind of exciting images he needed for his film and travelogues. Leaving Woodward at Kikori, Hurley went to Kairuku Island to join Father Bach of the Sacred Heart Mission for a tour of mission stations in the mountains behind Hall Sound as far as Ononge. This was Hurley's first experience of inland Papua.

The patrol gave him insights into the differences between the Protestant and Catholic approaches to missionary work. Although the former had been hospitable and cooperative, he had found their unbending dogmatism and general approach lacking the practicality and foresight of the Catholics. The Catholics received praise in his diaries; for the Protestants he reserved some trenchant criticisms. The patrol also exposed him to cultures which lacked the massive architecture and spectacular art forms of the Gulf of Papua.

Back in Port Moresby, Murray invited him to stay at Government House. These last few days of the first expedition saw Hurley developing very friendly relationships with some of the government officials. Bell, Commissioner for Native Affairs, gave him "a very fine native lakatoi" (Diary D, 18 August 1921), probably a model of the large trading canoes used by the Motu people of the Port Moresby area for their trading voyages (*hiri*) to the Gulf of Papua. Hurley departed for Sydney "well disposed towards the administration . . . ." and full of friendship and respect for Murray, though he was acutely aware of the enmity expressed towards Murray by many of the white population of Port Moresby. Some of these had petitioned King George V in 1920 for Murray's removal from office. They were unsuccessful, and the incident did nothing to improve relations between them and Murray. For a while Hurley saw himself as a possible mediator between Murray and his opponents, and had considered approaching a visiting Australian parliamentarian for support. Perhaps fortunately for all concerned, the opportunity for intervention did not arise.

THE SECOND EXPEDITION OF 1922-1923.

Back in Australia, Hurley prepared the first version of his film *Pearls and Savages*. While it had some good footage, it lacked the dramatic scenes and excitement that he wanted. His visit to Kikori and the Purari area, and stories about peoples to the west, promised him the material he needed, and so he began planning a second expedition for 1922-1923. This was to be very differently executed from that of 1920-1921. He had learned the difficulties of relying on others for transport and accommodation, and the rigors of undertaking an expedition by himself. The second expedition would be more scientifically oriented and better equipped.

The first expedition had been well publicised in Sydney through his articles in *The Sun* newspaper, as well as by his film and lecture presentations. For the second expedition Hurley formed a company of leading Sydney citizens who received a quarter share in the world rights of the film he was to produce in return for £4,000 invested in the expedition. It is not clear how much money was raised in this manner, but not all assistance was in the form of cash. Mr Lebbeus Hordern of Sydney loaned two biplane aircraft: a Curtiss 'Seagull' flying-boat and a Short 'Shrimp' biplane seaplane. Ex-RAF flyer Captain Andrew Lang was engaged as pilot, with A.J. Hill as mechanic. Hurley had recognised the potential of flying machines for Papuan exploration in 1921 during his visit to Kikori, when he noted in his diary that the best view of the delta country around Kikori could only be obtained from the air. Woodward had assisted Hurley's desire for panoramic views by setting a party of government convicts to clear more than a hectare of bush on the top of Aird Hills. The resulting panorama was reasonably satisfactory, but not as good as an aerial photograph; moreover, in the flat delta areas of the Gulf of Papua, high ground was available only at Aird Hills. Hurley hoped to use the planes for both aerial surveys and exploration. According to Sinclair (1978:12), Hurley intended to use the 'Shrimp' out of Daru to explore the south coast of Irian Jaya and to survey Torres Strait, while the 'Seagull' would make a crossing of the island of New Guinea from south to north. Neither project eventuated.

To complete his team Hurley approached the Australian Museum for the services of A.R. McCulloch to make biological and ethnographic collections for the Museum. McCulloch was a particularly useful addition to the team, with extensive field experience in the Pacific and a broad biological knowledge; he had also had some experience in movie photography while on Lord Howe Island. Later, in Port Moresby, Hurley obtained administration approval for the Assistant Government Anthropologist, F.E. Williams, to join the party on its visit to Lake Murray.

The funding permitted Hurley to hire a vessel to act as transport and field base for the team while in Papua. The boat was to be equipped with a wireless provided by Amalgamated Wireless of Australasia and an electricity generator. Hurley's own equipment is not detailed in the diaries, but included a phonograph in addition to the camera gear.

The expedition thus started, on paper at least, as probably the best equipped, best staffed and reasonably well funded private expedition to Papua up to that time. Lang and Hill arrived in Port Moresby with the Curtiss 'Seagull' in August 1922, and Lang made the first test flight on 5 September, the day before Hurley and McCulloch arrived with the 'Shrimp' and other equipment. The 'Shrimp' was successfully flown on 8 September.

Hurley found a mixed reception among the white population of Port Moresby. The planters, in particular, resented comments he had made about them in his articles in *The Sun*. But the administration staff was generally very helpful and cooperative, and Murray invited Hurley and McCulloch to stay with him at Government House. The Wireless Station provided McCulloch with assistance in the handling of the wireless, for which he would have responsibility throughout the expedition. The team was also loaned weapons from the government armoury, and was able to draw on government stock for certain supplies. But Hurley's plans soon ran into difficulties.

The boat owners of Port Moresby were aware of the wealthy sponsors and assumed that it was a sellers' market; they asked up to £300 per month for the hire of a vessel. Hurley needed a vessel for three months and could not afford such a high rate. He eventually secured the *Kerema*, an old and poorly maintained vessel, for £30 per month. The low fee, however, was a false economy and he was obliged to spend a considerable sum on repairs, thus delaying the start of the expedition. Some of this time was spent flying, and visiting islands offshore from Port Moresby.

While camping on Daugo Island, they received a letter from the Official Secretary advising them that they were camped in the quarantine area, and that the area would be used to isolate some cases of mumps on a Burns Philp ship; Hurley and McCulloch must, therefore, move camp. Hurley's response to this was "irate and amused"; another passenger from the same ship was a guest at Government House, showing an unexplained inconsistency (Diary 1, 22 September 1922).

McCulloch finally left Port Moresby for the Purari delta on 3 October on the *Kerema*, now renamed the *Eureka*. Hurley left two days later with Lang in the 'Seagull'. The two parties met at Kaimari where they remained for two weeks. During this time the 'Seagull' deteriorated, its wood and canvas structure being unable to withstand the adverse tropical conditions. Williams joined the team on 19 October, two days before the expedition departed for Daru, where Hurley sent Lang and Hill back to Sydney by boat with the 'Seagull'. Lang and Hill, constantly at loggerheads, were morose, depressing companions, and Hurley was glad to be rid of them from the team. There seems also to have been some friction between Hurley and Williams, for Williams left the party at Daru. To add further to their problems the *Eureka's* engine and pump kept breaking down, largely as a result of the incompetence of the engineer, Bell, who had failed to overhaul the engine properly before leaving Port Moresby, and also had failed to purchase any spare parts. All in all, while Hurley had obtained some excellent photographs at Kaimari, and McCulloch had been able to purchase artefacts and collect biological specimens, the expedition had started rather poorly. The trip up the Fly River to Lake Murray lifted Hurley's spirits and, apart from continued engine failures, the rest of the expedition went comparatively smoothly until the team returned to Port Moresby.

In Port Moresby many people had heard of the expedition's exploits, some of which McCulloch had relayed via wireless to *The Sun* in Sydney. These reports sought to be sensational and embellished fact, it seems, if they are compared with Hurley's diary entries. However, Hurley and McCulloch seemed to have been unprepared for the effect these reports had on people in Port Moresby and had to spend some time setting the record straight.

Far more serious for the expedition was an order from the Acting Official Secretary, on behalf of Staniforth Smith who was serving as Administrator of the colony while Murray was on leave, which impounded all of the expedition's collections. Apparently Hurley had already received notification that a consignment of specimens sent by McCulloch from Daru had been impounded, and now learned the reason. While on Lake Murray he had photographed members of his party carrying guns while inspecting a deserted longhouse. He had shown these photographs to a missionary who had reported to the

Resident Magistrate at Daru that he thought Hurley was using force to obtain specimens. Staniforth Smith felt that an investigation should be held, and requested the Resident Magistrate to carry out inquiries on Lake Murray. The collections were removed from the *Eureka* on 16 January and were deposited in the Port Moresby museum. Hurley insisted that statements be taken from all members of his expedition to refute the accusations. McCulloch also produced correspondence which showed that not only had the expedition obtained all necessary collecting permits, but had an agreement with the administration that the collections would be shipped to Sydney where items required for the official Papuan Collection, housed at the Australian Museum, would be transferred. The matter generated much bad will between Hurley and the administration officials and he left Port Moresby for Sydney on 26 January with the matter unresolved.

In Sydney Hurley made as much publicity out of the matter as he could, and there developed an exchange of letters and articles in *The Sun* which became, to say the least, acrimonious (Purse 1980). Murray finally released most of the collections, but some items were returned to Kaimari. Williams apparently disapproved of Hurley's actions there in obtaining photographs, and of McCulloch's in purchasing artefacts. He raised the matter again in a special Anthropological Report published by the administration (Williams 1923a). In many of his actions, however, Hurley seems to have followed practices he had observed of government officers. While this does not excuse him in any way, he saw himself acting in a manner consistent with the attitudes of many white people at that time. When the artefact collection finally reached Sydney, a number of artefacts were transferred to the official Papuan Collection. Despite the final altercation with the Papuan administration, and the other problems encountered during the expedition, Hurley rated the expedition a resounding success, and photographically it was.

The difficulties with the Papuan administration had nothing to do with permits for collecting or for export. On his first expedition Hurley had been unaware of the need to obtain a permit to collect and export artefacts, and the many artefacts he collected appear to have been confiscated, though he made no reference to this in his diaries. For the second expedition he intended to be better prepared and sought the assistance of Charles Anderson, Director of the Australian Museum, in obtaining a permit. He informed Anderson that "I neglected to obtain such authority during my last visit with the result that I was debarred from securing relics that would have been of great value and interest to the Museum" (Australian Museum Archives H42/22: Hurley to Anderson, 1 July 1922). Anderson approached the Prime Minister's Department in Melbourne and was advised that Hurley should get the permit when in Port Moresby. Anderson received a telegram from the Official Secretary in Port Moresby to the effect that Hurley and McCulloch would be granted a permit to "collect specimens not required by the Papuan Government and referring to ordinances regarding export of animals". McCulloch took the telegram with him and the permit was issued; McCulloch also obtained a special licence to permit him to collect bird of paradise skins, up to 50 of each species, largely because some headdresses incorporated them.

DISPOSAL OF THE TORRES STRAIT-PAPUA NEGATIVE COLLECTION

Prior to the 1922-1923 expedition, Hurley had advised Anderson that the Museum could purchase prints of the first expedition through Kodak Australasia at trade rates: "The same will also apply to the subjects of my new venture" (Australian Museum Archives H4/22: Hurley to Anderson, 12 June 1922). But when *The Jungle Woman* was completed, he decided to dispose of the collection, perhaps because he felt that his involvement with the area was ended. He wrote to Anderson offering the collection to the Museum for £100; he had been offered £500 by an American museum, but preferred that the collection remain in Australia. His letter to Anderson implies that the entire collection of glass negatives from the two expeditions was being offered, but that was not so. The Museum agreed to the purchase price and received 1,120 negatives, although Hurley regarded 54 of them as duplicates. At least a further 140 negatives were later deposited in the National Library of Australia in Canberra with many of Hurley's papers. The Canberra collection includes many from the book *Pearls and Savages*, and some used for publicity purposes and press articles. Since Hurley himself recorded having taken more than 1,200 negatives on the 1920-1921 expedition, and at least another 600 were taken on the second expedition, these two collections do not account for the total taken. The location of the balance is not known.

In addition to offering the collection to the Australian Museum, Hurley appears to have made a similar offer to Murray in Papua "for the Canberra Museum", presumably meaning that they could be kept with the official Papuan Collection of artefacts (which were in fact still held in Sydney at the Australian Museum). Murray's response is not known. Thorpe, Ethnologist at the Australian Museum, strongly recommended to Anderson that the offer be accepted: "In the opinion of your servant, the collection of negatives, together with the loan of the diaries is of inestimable scientific value...." (Australian Museum Archives 389/27: Thorpe to Anderson, undated March 1927).

The negatives included many stereo pairs from both

Torres Strait and Papua and colour negatives from Torres Strait; Hurley did not indicate in his notes on the collection what happened to the colour negatives taken on Mailu Island in Papua.

The negatives identified as being in colour were the results of an additive colour method known as the Finlay process. The essential imaging component still remained a standard panchromatic black and white plate but during exposure a coloured screening plate was placed in front of it. The resulting negative was processed normally, then contact printed to make a positive black and white image. This positive would then be sandwiched with a coloured screening plate in register, and taped together. The final colour image was then ready for viewing or for the printer's plate making. While the system sounds clumsy and time consuming compared with today's relatively easy colour production, the Finlay process at least had the advantage of a stable black and white negative which contributed greatly to image durability over the years in storage.

Under the terms of the sale, Hurley surrendered any further claim on the negatives; they could be used unconditionally and without restriction by the Museum. His loan of the field diaries was, however, conditional. They contain many passages of a personal nature which he felt should be kept confidential. However, he permitted the Museum to copy any passages relating to the photographs and anthropological topics. These extracts could be "published or used for publication in the Museum magazine" (Australian Museum Archives 389/27: Hurley to Wells, 23 May 1927). The Museum promptly prepared a set of 12 postcards from some of the negatives, with captions prepared by Thorpe from the diary extracts. The diaries were returned to Hurley and were eventually deposited in the National Library of Australia, Canberra.

Among the artefacts received by the Museum through Hurley and McCulloch was a rack for the display of human skulls from Urama Island. Hurley had the rack made especially for the Museum, and had negotiated the purchase of some skulls, *kwoi* boards and crocodile skulls. In depositing this at the Museum he set a condition that the Trust must display it, and not leave it in the reserve collection. The Museum constructed a much-reduced version of an Urama men's house, using "thatch-palm leaves" from Lord Howe Island as the roofing material. The skull rack was set up at the front of the house. Hurley and McCulloch had not been able to obtain enough skulls to fill the rack, and so the rack was completed by using skulls from all over the world from the Museum's collections.

The Trust more than fulfilled the condition; the exhibit was opened in January 1926 and was finally dismantled in 1976. During the dismantling it was found that much of the original framework had been replaced by plaster of Paris casts, painted to simulate the original. This probably reflects the destruction or damage of the original materials by insects while the artefacts were impounded in Port Moresby.

McCulloch did not live to see the acquisition of the negatives by the Museum, nor the opening of the Urama men's house display, for which he had organised the thatching. On his return to Australia his health deteriorated, and he had several long absences on sick leave. His medical certificates on file at the Australia Museum show that during 1923 and 1924 he was suffering from malaria and dysentery, both possibly resulting from the Papuan expedition. He recovered and in 1925 attended a conference in Hawaii. While there he committed suicide. A memorial to him was later erected on Lord Howe Island.

HURLEY AS A RECORDER

Frank Hurley was first and foremost a photographer, but we are fortunate that the images were not his sole concern. On all of his major ventures he kept daily diaries recording events, people, places and general impressions. These written records are important adjuncts to the photographs and films, and they provided the main sources for his many newspaper articles, travelogues and books. Much of his published material consists of direct quotations from or paraphrases of, diary entries. *Pearls and Savages* is said to have been prepared in a New York hotel room with Hurley dictating to a team of stenographers. This task was eased by the use of many sections taken from the diaries. This does not detract from the value of his publications, but draws attention to the certainty with which he regarded the accuracy of the diary information.

When Hurley allowed the Australian Museum access to his diaries he stated that most of the information of an ethnographic nature had been obtained from missionaries and, therefore, was reliable. Not all the information, however, came from missionaries; government officers, planters and others also provided advice. Hurley did not always identify his sources, but he did note when the information came through interpreters or was based on his own observations and interpretations. In some cases he stated openly in the diaries that he was uncertain of the accuracy of his statements, or that he had received conflicting information and what he recorded was the version he thought might be the most accurate one.

Hurley, however, was not concerned with detail; he was recording general information which would be used for general audiences. The most detailed account of an area is that provided for Mailu Island, where he seems to have had access, perhaps through Saville, to a paper published by Malinowski (1915). Here, he quoted verbatim from Malinowski's text, or extensively paraphrased passages. He was puzzled by the attempt of F.E. Williams, to obtain detailed information on some ritual objects at Kaimari. He found Williams' concern for accuracy time consuming and rather irritating. Williams, however, was preparing a major study of the Namau people of the Purari delta, and was writing for a professional audience which would insist on higher standards and more detail than were necessary for Hurley's purposes.

Given Hurley's approach and the limitations which faced him, he was remarkably successful in minimising errors of fact. He certainly made a mess of his initial description of Motu pottery manufacture, but these errors were corrected in a later entry (see V.4422). He had no anthropological or linguistic training, and can be forgiven for errors made in recording the names of people, places or artefacts. Most of these were subsequently checked and corrected where necessary before they were used in his book.

The diaries provide some interesting insights into the authenticity of some photographs. Many of the traditional events recorded by both still and movie photography were staged for Hurley. The purist may object to the lack of authenticity on the grounds that, as reconstructions of activities, they lack value for showing contexts, etc. But it must be remembered that some of the scenes have never been recorded photographically elsewhere; they remain our only visual accounts. Yet we must regard the photographs, to some degree, as constructions of how Hurley required the scenes to be presented to him, and treat their content with some caution. The Motuan girl carrying a water pot (V.4466) is wearing a wealth of traditional valuables for an everyday task. The photograph was posed and he probably asked her to wear the ornaments. A similar, more obvious, case comes from Kerewa village on Goaribari Island, where he photographed one woman three times wearing different ornaments and waist cloths (V. 4223). On Urama Island he went even further and arranged the interior of the men's house to his liking. We must bring a critical mind to the interpretation of these photographs. Hurley is not presenting us with the world as it presented itself to him; he has modified it slightly, perhaps on occasion misleadingly, to obtain the best possible image.

During his time as a war photographer, Hurley experienced much criticism from some quarters for his composite photographs, in which details from several negatives were combined on one photograph. The Papuan negatives contain several examples of this approach in which clouds have been added to a scene, or a flight of flying foxes has been placed over a longhouse (the former is held by the Australian Museum, the latter by the National Library of Australia). None of these is included in this selection.

THE SELECTION

This volume contains less than ten per cent of Hurley's collection, and is restricted to Papua. No selection is likely to receive approval from everyone, and in making the choices we have been very conscious of this fact. We have not tried to select only the technically best negatives. Our concern is to show some of those, together with negatives which have anthropological, historical and artistic quality. Neither have we attempted to achieve a numerical balance for each area. The collection covers some areas more extensively than others, reflecting the length of time he spent at any location as well as the interest he found there.

The images presented here are taken directly from the original negatives complete with minor blemishes which reflect not upon Hurley's competence but on the difficult conditions under which he was working. Most of the images have been cropped, but only in a few cases have they been touched up to remove the worst of the blemishes. For each photograph we give its registration number in the Photography Department at the Australian Museum. We also provide a commentary, frequently drawing on quotations from Hurley's original diaries held by the National Library of Australia in Canberra. These diary extracts are presented as Hurley originally wrote them, complete with errors of grammar and spelling. It must be remembered that most of the diary entries were written late at night, after a full day's work, and often after an evening spent in developing film and plates. Others were written on board the *Eureka* during rough weather, when literary excellence was not Hurley's main concern. In only a few instances were entries made more than a day later than the events they recorded. While the quotations preserve Hurley's original spellings for place names, elsewhere the orthography presented in the *Papua New Guinea Gazetteer* (Papua New Guinea Place Names Committee 1974) has been used.

Neither the photographs nor the commentaries present an integrated theme on anthropological or historical topics. For any one photograph several different commentaries could be written, each highlighting a different aspect of the image or the circumstances under which it was recorded. There is, however, a continuous theme; it is Hurley himself who provides it.

Jim Specht,
*Division of Anthropology,
Australian Museum, Sydney.*

There is a curious tradition with books about famous photographers of always including technical information on how the photographs were made. Rarely do we see or read what maul and chisel were used by the sculptor, and what brush or paints on the palette were used by the painter. Cameras, film and formulae are only tools to the photographer, nothing more. Logically, our concerns should be about the images themselves and the person making them, not with the tool kit.

Not surprisingly one finds few remarks devoted to technique or equipment in the diaries of Frank Hurley. Most often the entries record working situations or the reminding list of processing times for his films and plates. It is perhaps appropriate to include a number of the entries and with some imagination we can begin to appreciate the conditions under which the man was working.

In the evening of 17 October 1922, Hurley developed 60 plates taken at Kaimari Village, on the Purari River delta, using muddy river water. Photographically he was satisfied with their quality, but:

I am however much troubled by the appearance of small blisters while drying the negatives. These appear to be caused by the water. There is not the slightest appearance of blisters when the negatives are put to dry but by the morning several plates have been covered with them. Happily, most of the subjects I have been able to take over, and those too bad are recorded on film. I notice a minute black dot in the centre of each bubble, which appears to be foreign matter from the river water. (Diary 1, 17 October 1922)

The problem persisted and Hurley had to abandon any hope of developing the exposed film and plates until fresh clean water was available:

The film appears to be tough and faultless when set up to dry, but by morning immense numbers of clear spots form. Several negatives were utterly ruined. Under the microscope it would appear that the river water impurities deposit on the film and form the Neucleii (sic) of these spots. I intend doing no further developing until suitable water can be secured. (Diary 1, 19 October 1922)

Throughout both expeditions Hurley had problems with water temperatures. On Lake Murray he found the water far too warm at 90° - 92°F (Diary 2, 16 November 1922), and there was no way to reduce the temperature. On the previous expedition he had been able to obtain ice on Thursday Island, but ice was not readily available at most white settlements. At other times, rain might lower water temperature sufficiently for Hurley to process his plates and film. He devised a formula to assist the developing process.

Frequently the developer rises to 87 degrees. I find that the addition of 4oz formalin to 8 gallons solution assists the toughening during development. I reduce the fixing temperature by dissolving a quantity of Hypo in the bath and make a combined hardening and fixing bath by the addition of 3oz chrome alum plus 2lb Pot. Metabisulphite to ten gallons water. The first washing is effected in a weak alum bath. After which a ten minute washing with hypo eliminater (permanganate potash) completes the process. After all these precautions the film will probably reticulate in the drying and the result of ones hard earned efforts is a failure. To develop 6 frames each of 65 feet takes three hours. (Diary A, 26 December 1920)

Even when problems such as these were overcome, there were other, unexpected, hazards. On Mabuiag cockroaches ate the emulsion while the film was drying (Diary A, 26 January 1921), and on Lake Murray a crocodile attacked and destroyed about 100 feet of film which was being washed in the lake (Diary 2, 16 November 1922).

These quotations provide an insight into the shaping of the legacy of images made by Hurley in Papua. This legacy, in the form of more than eleven hundred half plate and quarter plate negatives held in the photographic archive of the Australian Museum, remains a testimony to one of Australia's most remarkable photographers.

The selection of photographs in this book, some of which are Hurley's finest, provides ample evidence for his acclaim. The full value and understanding of his contribution can only be measured against the inexorable passage of time. However fragile the ageing glass negatives may be, the subjects portrayed on them are forever timeless. Those who will journey through these pages and view these photographs, are viewing them as Hurley wanted them seen. Remember, too, that photographs are not reality but the selections of an individual's perception of a reality. It is this that transcends the commonplace, and for this, we celebrate these photographs and the man who made them.

John Fields,
Photography Department,
Australian Museum, Sydney.

Photographs of the 1920-1923 Expeditions

V.4404 *Hanuabada and Elevala villages, at low tide, near Port Moresby, National Capital District.*

The date of this photograph is unknown. It is taken from the top of the hill on the small island of Elevala looking towards the mainland and the group of four villages generally called Hanuabada but more correctly known as Poreporena (Seligmann 1910: 45-7; Belshaw 1957; Groves 1963). Elevala village is in the foreground.

These villages have mostly Motu-speaking populations, though there is one section inhabited by Koita speakers. The Motu, a sea-oriented people, traditionally lacked adequate garden land on the mainland and traded with the Koita for vegetables. Some Koita lived near Motu settlements and adopted many Motu customs. The Motu are divided into three groups. The Hanuabada-Elevala Motu belong to the 'Western' group.

After arranging my official itinerary, I walked round to the two native villages, HANUABADA village and ELEVARA village, about two miles distant. These villages are of remarkable interest on account of their having been built out into the shallow water. Hanuabada village comprises over a hundred native huts, built up on lanky piles. Communication is linked with Elevara by means of a narrow bridge way, built about 15 feet above high tide. On either side of this narrow footway, plank tracks lead to the houses. The villages are laid out much as if on land, only the whole communication ways and houses are above the water. In front of each house is a platform-like verandah, where the art of making pottery is carried on. Behind the platform is a narrow sheltered verandah and then the house. The whole arrangement, with its waterways between the houses on which float many canoes, is intensely pictorial though its fragility and ricketyness gave me qualms at every footstep. (Diary B, 1 April 1921)

The small canoe in the foreground, with an outrigger, is for local coastal work. To its left and behind to the right are the massive hulls (*asi*) of the *lagatoi*, the multi-hulled ocean-going canoes used for the trading voyages (*hiri*) to villages in the Gulf of Papua (see V.4422).

Seligmann (1910: frontispiece) provides a view of Elevala taken from the hill above Hanuabada, also showing *lagatoi* hulls. Of Hanuabada, Hurley wrote:

The village houses are built up on high sticks about 12 feet above high tides. The first row is practically on the shore, excepting at high tide, and faces on to a large cleared space fringed with coconuts. Here the children play, canoes are rigged and overhauled, and the work of burning pottery, which is the work of the women, is done. Behind this front row of dwellings lies another built in the shallow water, and the houses are approached by rickety bridgeways and planks, that spring about and threaten to dislodge and precipitate the crosser into the mud. (Diary D, 11 August 1921)

V.4404

V.4405 *Main walkway in Elevala village, near Port Moresby, National Capital District. 15-16 August 1921?*

The date of this photograph is uncertain since Hurley visited the Hanuabada-Elevala area on several occasions on both expeditions.

I devoted some time to the village of Elevala which is built on the less exposed side of a small island and is connected to Tanobada by a small treacherous bridge. The villages of Elevala are built upon long piles over shallow water; they face one another and access to them is by means of a shady roadway of saplings and logs supported on a level with the house platforms. The narrow bridge which connects the terminal of this raised road, beneath which the current sweeps, spans an exposed gap over water rough with the wild wind that has been raging all day. The force of the wind almost blew me into the ditch as I crossed the hazardous track which swayed and creaked. (Diary D, 11 August 1921)

Tanobada is one of the four settlements covered by the general name Hanuabada (Poreporena) (Seligmann 1910: 45).

V.4405

V.4422 *Pottery manufacture at Hanuabada village, National Capital District. 16 August 1921.*

Hanuabada, the 'great village', is situated a few kilometres west of Port Moresby and belongs to the 'Western Motu' group of villages, together with its immediate neighbour, Elevala. Pottery manufacture, for both local consumption and for trade, was still a major activity at the time of Hurley's visits to Port Moresby in 1920-21 and 1922-23. Each year the Motu potters produced thousands of pots for trade with villages in the Gulf of Papua in exchange for sago and other goods (Barton 1910; Dutton 1982).

During his 1920-21 expedition to Papua, Hurley recorded the process of pottery making twice. On the first occasion he may have written his diary comments from verbal information only, since his account contains several gross errors. This photograph was taken in August, at the end of the expedition, when he was able to observe the total process. At the time, there was probably a great deal of pottery making in the Motu villages as preparations for the annual trading voyage (*hiri*) to the Gulf of Papua were well under way. The '*lakatoi*' (*lagatoi*) referred to in the second extract were the large multi-hulled sailing canoes used for the *hiri*.

Native pottery manufacture is carried on extensively, and these villages have acquired much fame for their art. A local red clay is used and after a process of laborious grinding and puddling is kneaded into a fine dough-like mass. A round stone about five inches in diameter and a small spatula are the only tools employed for the fashioning. Water pots appear to be the principal utensils made. The bottom is first fashioned, much in shape as shown, the stone being used as a form for the inside and the spatula kept moistened, presses the clay into form against it. The bottoms when formed are put into the sun to dry and then burnt by simply piling wood around them and firing. The tips are then moulded and formed onto the bottoms and fired again. A dark brown stain is imparted by pounding up mangrove bark into a thick tan coloured juice and dashing it with a small brush onto the hot utensils just after they have been withdrawn from the firing. This pottery is a form of currency, and Lakatois (canoes) filled with a cargo, sail up to the delta country and barter their wares for sago, which grows there in great profusion. (Diary B, 1 April 1921)

The two-stage construction and firing process did not exist. Hurley may have been misled by the use of old broken vessels to support pots under construction. His observation of pottery making at the end of his 1920-21 expedition is both more complete and accurate.

Morning to Hanuabada village to illustrate the making of earthen pots. The process is as follows. The clay is dug from small pits in the hillsides nearby, and is carried in by the women, who pound it with a stone on a piece of board (generally a piece of a canoe side). The pounded clay is picked over for small stones and grit and when freed of such foreign inclusions, salt water is poured on and the clay is kneaded with a small percentage of sand. When brought to the right consistency, a lump is placed on a base generally the broken top section of a pot. The clay is gradually worked up first in a hollow cylinder, then wider, like a common flower pot and then the shaping begins. By using a large pebble for a form inside the pot, and beating the side of the pot against it with a small flat "pat", the vessel takes up a globular form of splendid symmetry. A lip is formed around the mouth, the whole appearing like a fish globe but without a flat bottom. The clay pots are put in the sun to dry for a day and then baked. This is done by placing the pots in a line, their mouths facing into the wind, and then covering them around with small dry sticks laid vertically side by side. The fire, under the influence of the wind, drives into the pot and around it, after half an hour's baking the pot is withdrawn, and mangrove bark pulped and boiled in water, making a dark tan solution, is swish brushed on. The pot is then replaced in the fire for a few minutes and is withdrawn. Generally the vessel is of conventional form and undecorated. The pots form one of the principal articles of trade with the people of the mud villages of Kaimare and Purari. Lakatois sail to the delta laden with pots towards the end of the S.E. monsoon. They exchange their earthen wares for sago which grows in vast profusion amidst the delta swamps, and return in their lakatoi's when the North West trades set in. Pots are only made by women, the trading is done exclusively by the men. (Diary D, 16 August 1921)

V.4422

V.4466 *Girl of Hanuabada village carrying a water pot.*

The date of this photograph is not known. Hurley visited Hanuabada on several occasions on each of his expeditions, particuarly when he was a guest at Government House with the Lieutenant-Governor, J.H.P. Murray.
   Built over the shallows near the shore, Hanuabada had no readily available fresh water supply. The women had to transport it from the mainland in earthenware pots which seem to have had short lives, for Hurley noted that the potters of Hanuabada were making mainly water pots (Diary B, 1 April 1921).
   It is probable that this woman was specially posed for the photograph, since it is unlikely that she would wear so many shell valuables for an every day task.

V.4409 *Two girls of Elevala village, near Port Moresby, National Capital District. 2 April 1921?*

On 2 April 1921, Hurley recorded in his diary that he visited Hanuabada in the afternoon to photograph 'types'. This photograph may be from that session or from one of 16 August, 1921 when he photographed a dance at Hanuabada arranged for him by the Resident Magistrate at Port Moresby, Mr J.T. O'Malley. Of the dancers Hurley noted:

A pleasant feature was the girls, who in lines in front and behind the dancers, kept time by a body swing which caused their grass skirts to move in a pleasant rhythmic way. Many of these girls are extremely pretty, and of proportions that would exact the envy of many of our own women. (Diary D, 16 August 1921)

The girl on the left is wearing a curved boar's tusk (*doa*) hung from a *tautau* necklace of shell discs. The girl on the right wears a *toea* arm ring of *Conus millepunctatus* on her left arm, and a *mairi* shell crescent round her neck over several necklaces. The *doa, tautau* and *toea* are important valuables which feature in ceremonial displays and exchanges such as the ceremony for the first-born child, bride-price, and in feasts between two men competing in the *Hekara* (Koita: *Hekarai*) as a means of settling a dispute (Seligmann 1910; Groves 1954).

V.4415 *Girl of Elevala village, near Port Moresby, National Capital District. 2 April 1921?*

This photograph may have been taken on the same day as V.4409. The girl is wearing a *toea* shell arm ring on each arm, a *mairi* shell crescent round her neck, and several necklaces of dogs' teeth (*dodoma*). Above the *toea* are woven vegetable fibre arm rings into which have been thrust ornamental plants.

Traditionally, a large *toea* would purchase a large parcel of sago (*gorugoru*) weighing 100-150 kilograms from villages in the Gulf of Papua during the *hiri* trading expeditions. *Mairi* shell crescents and *tautau* shell necklaces also purchased sago, but the *toea* could also be used to purchase the massive logs from which the Motu men would make new hulls for their *lagatoi* trading canoes (Seligmann 1910: 109,115).

The name *toea* has been adopted for the basic unit of cash currency in Papua New Guinea (100 *toea* equal 1 *kina*).

V.4415

V.4413 *Girl of Elevala village, near Port Moresby, National Capital District.*

Whereas V.4409 and V.4415 were taken on land, this photograph seems to have been taken within Elevala village. The girl is wearing a necklace of fish vertebrae and possible sea-urchin spines or seed-cases.

V.4413

V.4431 *Platform* dubu *at Hanuabada, near Port Moresby, National Capital District.*

Hurley spent considerable time in the Hanuabada area on both expeditions. It is impossible to determine when this photograph was taken, for the diaries do not mention a *dubu*.

According to Seligmann (1910: 17-23, 60-65), platform *dubu* were more typical of the Koita people than of the Motu. Oral traditions of the Sinagoro speakers east of the Motu claim that the platform *dubu* originated in their area. In some areas on the south coast of Papua, the *dubu* took the form of a house. At the time Seligmann wrote his book, *dubu* were already rare among both the Koita and Motu, presumably reflecting mission influences.

The platform *dubu* provided a focal point for the ceremonial life of the Koita, with each lineage erecting one for its own use. It was basically a two-storey rectangular platform supported by carved posts and horizontal beams. The *dubu* provided a meeting place for men to discuss serious matters, and for a man who has successfully killed another to display himself. The platform was regarded as being to a limited extent sacred, with the spirits of the dead occupying it at certain times. Only during the ceremony called by Seligmann (1910: 145-50) the "*tabu* feast" were women allowed on the platform, when they would participate in the dancing. During this ceremony a new *dubu* would be built if the old one was unsafe to support dancers, and large quantities of food were displayed around the *dubu*. The *tabu* feast appears to have been designed to placate malicious mythical beings who occupied specific localities. Their power was sufficient to cause sickness or death to anyone who visited these areas (Seligmann 1910: 183-6).

This *dubu* may have belonged to the Koita section of Hanuabada.

V.4461 *Male dancers at Hanuabada, near Port Moresby, National Capital District. 16 August 1921?*

At the end of his first expedition, Hurley observed a dance at Hanuabada which had been specially staged for him through the assistance of the Resident Magistrate in Port Moresby, Mr J.T. O'Malley. This photograph was probably taken on that occasion.

The men are wearing *toea, doa, tautau* and *dodoma* ornaments, in addition to their feather, shell and turtle-shell decorated headdresses. Some of these feathers probably came from the Koiari people, inland behind the Koita, but the Koita also formerly obtained feathers from people to the west (Seligmann 1910: 94). The men are also wearing painted strips of bark cloth at their waists.

Dances played a most important role among the Motu (Groves 1954).

Individual men of status and wealth would sponsor a dance, calling on other members of their lineage to provide support. Dances were usually linked with feasts at which much food was distributed, thereby signifying the social strength and wealth of the sponsor. No trading voyage (*hiri*) could start without the appropriate dances being held, including one on the *lagatoi* themselves. Hurley did not record which dance was performed for him:

The natives certainly attired themselves admirably. Several wore splendid head-dresses with fine paradise bird plumes, and were equal to any I have seen. In the dance the people became their old selves again, and devoid of European ramis and loin cloths they look vastly improved. The dance was perhaps monotonous, just moving to and fro, drumbarging and without any quick movement. Each dance to me appeared to have little variety and to see one was to see the lot. (Diary D, 16 August 1921)

V.4461

V.4395 *The Short 'Shrimp' being welcomed ashore at Port Moresby, National Capital District. 6 September 1922.*

On his first expedition to Papua in 1920-21, Hurley found that travel by boat and on foot posed severe limitations, especially given the limited time available to him. For the second expedition he was loaned two planes by Mr Lebbeus Hordern of Sydney: a Curtiss 'Seagull' biplane flying-boat, and a Short 'Shrimp' seaplane. The 'Seagull' travelled to Port Moresby on the Burns Philp ship *Marsina,* with the pilot, Captain Andrew Lang, and his mechanic, A.J. Hill, arriving on 17 August 1922. The 'Shrimp' travelled with Hurley and McCulloch on the *Morinda,* arriving on 6 September 1922, the day after Lang's first test flight of the 'Seagull'.

The test flight of 5 September caused consternation and amazement in Port Moresby, for this was the first plane ever seen there. The arrival of the 'Shrimp' on the following day generated no less interest:

A large crowd of natives had collected to see the new machine being landed and a large number of canoes came out from Hanuabada village decorated with fringes of stranded palm leaves in honour of the event. . . . .As the machine tipped the water the assembled natives gave throat to a prolonged war whoop and smote the canoe sides with their paddles, producing a deep noted boom. . . . . (Diary 1, 6 September 1922)

Within a week the planes had captured the imagination of the Motu children:

The popular village toy is now the aeroplane; and I must say that in the making of such toys, the native children are far ahead of the white. These aeroplane tops (sic) made by young boys were remarkably neat and accurate to detail. The propellers were made by cleverly twisting a strand of palm leaf and in the wind these rotated at a great spead. (Diary 1, 12 September 1922)

Hurley originally planned to use both planes to attempt a flight across New Guinea and to explore and survey the Papuan coast (Sinclair 1978: 12). These plans came to nothing. The 'Shrimp', called 'Fleetwings' by Hurley, flew only twice, on 8 and 11 September, and seems to have been left behind in Port Moresby when the party went into the Gulf of Papua with their vessel, the *Kerema* (renamed *Eureka* by Hurley), and the 'Seagull'. The severe tropical climate affected the 'Seagull's' fabric wing coverings, and it became unairworthy. Hurley was finally forced to send it back to Australia, a decision which he seems to have taken with relief, since Lang and Hill did not like each other, and Hurley found neither was congenial company, even though he respected their expertise. McCulloch wrote to Charles Anderson, Director of the Australian Museum on 25 October 1922 stating that. . . . ."Everything has so far been centred on the movements of the planes which have been a great responsibility to all, the district being very unsuitable for flying" (Museum Archives M62/22). Charles Hedley replied to McCulloch on 4 December 1922 that. . . . ."We were rather glad that the planes had to be discarded, as we feared that a mishap might occur and be a very serious affair for the whole party". (Museum Archives M62/22)

James Sinclair, in his *Wings of Gold* (1978: 12), discusses a problem with the number and identity of the planes loaned by Hordern. Hurley's diaries and photographs held by the Australian Museum and the National Library of Australia indicate only two planes: the 'Shrimp', registered G-AUPZ; and the 'Seagull', registered G-AUCU. Hordern had two 'Seagulls', the second with the registration G-AUCV. The latter, according to Sinclair, was the one which arrived in Port Moresby with Lang and Hill on 17 August 1922. Sinclair cites evidence that Lang was again in Port Moresby with 'Seagull' G-AUCV on 19 January 1923, more than two months after Hurley sent Lang and Hill with the 'Seagull' G-AUCU back to Thursday Island with funds to ship both themselves and the plane to Sydney. Prior to separating from Hurley's party, Hill gave Hurley a typed "Report on the condition of Curtiss Flying Boat G.AUCU", a copy of which is in Hurley's second diary for the 1922-23 expedition (3-5 November 1922). The record of G-AUCV arriving in Port Moresby on 17 August may be a misreading of poor handwriting or a typing error. It is possible that Lang returned to Sydney and took Hordern's second 'Seagull' G-AUCV back to Port Moresby in January 1923. Hurley was in Port Moresby at that time but makes no mention of Lang or the 'Seagull', though the poor relations between the two men and Hurley's problems with the administration over his collections may have led him to consider Lang's presence not worth a mention.

V.4398 *Aerial view of Tubusereia village, Central Province, photographed at an altitude of 300 metres. 18 September 1922.*

This is one of the first aerial photographs taken in Papua New Guinea.

Prior to departing from Port Moresby at the start of his second expedition, Hurley had both of his sea-planes, on loan from Mr Lebbeus Hordern of Sydney, tested to ensure mechanical safety and viability. His pilot, Captain Andrew Lang, flew the Short 'Shrimp' (registered number G-AUPZ), nicknamed the 'Fleetwings' by Hurley, on 8 and 11 September 1922. The Curtiss 'Seagull' flying-boat (registered number G-AUCU) was tested on 5 September, the day before Hurley arrived. On 18 September Hurley went up with Lang in the 'Seagull' to take the first aerial photographs.

They reached a maximum altitude of 925 metres over Bootless Bay, and at about 300 metres Hurley took "some very fine film of the various acquatic villages".

Tubusereia is a Motu village east of Port Moresby on Bootless Bay. Belonging to the 'Eastern Motu', Tubusereia did not participate in the annual trading voyage (*hiri*) from Port Moresby to the Gulf of Papua to exchange pottery and shell valuables for sago. Tubusereia did contribute, however, shell valuables, both made locally and imported from villages to the east, through exchange with Western Motu villages (Allen 1977; Dutton 1982).

Hurley did not visit Tubusereia, but his comments on Gaba Gaba are relevant:

This is one of the numerous villages along this coast which is built out in the shallow sea on piles nearby half a mile from land. Several inform me that the people, who are an acquatic race, have so erected their villages to isolate them from attack by the land tribes. . . . .Hygenically it has much to commend it and further the mosquito pest must be greatly minimised. (Diary B, 4 April 1921)

Since this photograph was taken the village has been mostly relocated to the mainland.

V.4468 *Display of food prior to a feast, Gabone Village, Central Province 1921.*

The village of Gabone stands on the edge of Marshall Lagoon. Hurley visited the village twice on his 1920-1921 expedition and was not impressed by the standards of cleanliness of the village and its inhabitants. He was, however, impressed by its "draught board pattern streets" and the display of food prior to a feast.

The houses made of mangrove stakes and thatched with grass resemble my humble illustration. Beneath the dome shaped sleeping compartment is built a floored platform where the dwellers pass most of their daily life, lousing and sleeping . . . A main thoroughfare passes along the crest of the ridge and the detached domiciles are built in rows on either side. From this main thoroughfare passage ways run at right angles and more dwellings. Communication to the upper sleeping apartment is had by a small ladder which passes up through a trap door entrance. (Diary B, 6 April 1921)

    Going up into the village, I was amazed to find high posts driven into the ground in front of the houses, and lining either side of the main thoroughfare, which runs across the main crest of the hill. Between the high posts which were between 40 and 50 feet high, and twelve paces apart, were lashed saplings at a height of 12 feet from the ground. From the ground to the top of the high posts Taro was fixed so as to make a thin spire of the vegetable. Along the saplings bunches of bananas were hung in an almost unbroken line. There were also great displays of native sago done up in a palm leaf. The main avenue was a striking festive display reminding one of the street exhibits at an agricultural show, only on a grander scale. It transpires that a feast, for exactly what purpose I do not know, is going to be held next Friday, by which time a large quantity of the food will have gone bad. (Diary C, 13 June 1921)

    This strange custom of displaying food before feasts accounts for the waste of immense quantities of good food. It is a mad custom that to me is unreasonable and incomprehensible. As at Mailu especially food is hard to grow, and it means tremendous waste of effort and time, it is a custom to be proscribed; also a taboo is placed on certain Coconuts and the nuts of these trees are allowed to fall unused for any purpose. Eating of them would make a person ill! (Diary C, 13 June 1921)

V.4477 *Woman in mourning, Vilirupu, Central Province. 12 June 1921.*

Hurley seems to have confused the names of an anchorage on Marshall Lagoon, a river that runs into the lagoon, and Gabone village. His diary relates his observations of mourners to Gabone village.

I also noticed many women in mourning — they being blackened from shaven head to foot, and wearing on their heads a sort of wreath made from the "Job's tear seeds". They also wore strings across each shoulder, passing in a cross over the breast and under the arms. One whom I photographed was wearing a small widow's cape. Ridiculous as the blackening with the mixture of charcoal, made by burning coconut husks and mixing with water, may seem, it is one of their most serious mourning customs, and any ridicule would at once drive the person indoors and miss a valuable subject. I have learned to look upon the native customs with interest, and what to them might appear approbation, and I find that by doing so one always wins them over to pose before the lens. (Diary C, 12 June 1921).

V.4477

37

V.4478 Hula village, Central Province. 13-14 June 1921.

Hula village is situated on Hood Point, about 90 kilometres southeast from Port Moresby. According to oral traditions, the Hula (Vulaa) arrived in the Hood Bay area about 200-250 years ago, and Hula village was established in the early 19th century (Oram 1968). Lacking land rights, the Hula occupied villages built on the reefs and gained their main subsistence through fishing and the exchange of fish for vegetables with land-based communities with gardens. The original inhabitants of the Hood Bay area, the Keapara (Kerepunu), and the Hula developed a mutually advantageous, if at times fragile, interdependency. The Hula were in frequent conflict with their neighbours and apparently conducted raids westwards into the Eastern Motu area. During the Motu *hiri,* Hula canoes would visit the Port Moresby area to supply the Motu who remained with fish in exchange for coconuts and vegetables.

The two aspects of conflict with their neighbours and lack of traditional lands were probably strong factors in the establishment of the villages on the reefs. In contrast to the Motu villages of Hanuabada and Elevala where the houses were linked by walkways, Hula village — like Tubusereia in V.4398 — consisted of free standing groups of houses with walkways only within each group.

Hurley visited Hula after his tour of mission stations on the north and south-east coasts of Papua in 1921. He observed:

Hula is a remarkable place. Oval shaped thatch roofs similar to Mailu, and in fact the other villages extending from Mailu to Hula along the coast, only the houses are built on high piles out over the water. A population of some 1000 people live in this acquatic village, which presents a remarkable sight, and is entirely cut off from the land. These people have followed the traditions of bygone times when their fathers and forefathers built their houses in this way for defence purposes. The attack would come from their land neighbours, who would have to make their way across the water and so be at a great disadvantage from those on top. If demolished they (the Hula) could put to sea in their large canoes, and so avoid further harassing, returning when the enemy had made off. Many of the houses have been modified to missionary ideas, and several are just square boxes roofed and walled with old iron sheets standing on poles. Mr. Bradbury, the L.M.S. Missionary, welcomed me on the beach, and has kindly invited me to stay with him and his wife. (Diary C, 13 June 1921)

Hurley later compared Hula with Hanuabada, where:

The houses are well built and it is remarkable that they have remained so long unaltered or disfigured by the usual scrap iron and bits of canvas. Hula village although some 40 miles from Port is ruined in this way. The women still wear grass skirts but most of the males wear a calico lavalava which degenerates their appearance, as it is generally filthy dirty and ragged. (Diary D, 11 August 1921)

V.4478

V.4505 *Mailu village, Amazon Bay, Central Province. 7-11 June 1921.*

On his first expedition, Hurley sailed on the *Tambar* in the company of Reverend and Mrs W.J.V. Saville who were returning to Mailu Island where Saville was running the London Missionary Society station. They formed an acquaintance and Hurley was invited to spend a few days on Mailu after his tour around the south-east and north coasts. They reached Mailu on 8 April:

We anchored off Mailu Island and I just had time to go ashore with the Savilles and take a few ocular and camera snapshots. (Diary B, 8 April 1921)

Saville subsequently (1926) published a descriptive ethnography about the Mailu people. Hurley's diary entries on his return visit in June 1921 are unusually detailed and comprehensive and contain many passages and paraphrases from Bronislaw Malinowski's (1915) study of the Mailu (Diary C, 9-10 June 1921). Hurley's primary reason, however, for returning to Mailu was not ethnographic:

The native village is just around the next bay. Several rows of domeshaped huts facing the beach in parallel rows. The island is encircled with a very beautiful coral reef and it is here that I hope to secure most of my colour plates of coral on my return journey. (Diary B, 8 April 1921)

While he obtained plates of the marine life, Hurley also became absorbed by the village itself:

Pictures present themselves at every turn and corner. The stately row of houses facing the beach, with the canoes riding in the shallow just off shore and the crab-claw sailed vessels coming and going is a glimpse of Papua as it was before the white man came. (Diary C, 9-10 June 1921)
    Mailu is the largest and most important village in the district. It was the most dreaded village by the mainland natives with whom it was almost constantly at war. The Mailu village consists of one compact group of houses, regularly built and arranged in two parallel rows with a street down the centre as in diagram. The street is about ten paces wide and the front line of houses faces onto the beach. The fronts of the houses face on to the street, but the row facing the beach appears also to have an extra front, whilst the row facing the plantation is entirely closed in. The streets are quite bare all grass having been trampled down, while the beach and sea front is lumbered with large canoes, the background of the large row of huts forming a fine effect to the seafront. (Diary C, 9-10 June 1921)

In *Pearls and Savages* (Hurley 1924: 47) is a similar view of Mailu, photographed through a natural rock archway. This plate is not held by the Australian Museum.

V.4489 *Mailu double-hulled canoe under sail, Central Province. 7-11 June 1921.*

The Mailu islanders are renowned as the major sea-borne traders of their area. Using large double-hulled sailing canoes, they linked commmunities to the east and west, acting as middlemen for the distribution of various goods along the coast. This annual series of trading voyages gave the Mailu access to wealth and prestige items as well as to foods. Hurley found the Mailu:

.... a hard unsympathetic lot whose sole aim and ambition appears to be to secure pigs — more pigs for their feasts. (Diary C, 11 June 1921)

The Mailu, a non-Austronesian language speaking people, are unusual in using a sea-going canoe style which is more often associated with Austronesian language speakers. Irwin (1978) has reviewed the archaeological evidences for the prehistory of Mailu and has argued for the gradual emergence of Mailu as the main pottery-producing and trading centre of the area. At some stage in this process the Mailu may have adopted the Austronesian form of double-hulled canoe.

The Mailu possess well proportioned sea-going canoes, provided with the well known crab-claw sail. I was told that the Mailu canoes are the best sea going canoes in the Territory, and as they can sail close to the wind, trading expeditions E and W are possible. From the fact that they are built of two dugouts in place of one they are able to stand heavy weather and carry a heavy cargo. The hull consists of two dugouts joined together by a set of poles, on which rests a platform. There is no differentiation between bow and stern, as it is sailed either way, but the hull is not bilaterally symmetrical, because one of the dugouts is larger than the other, and it is on the larger one that the mast is fixed.

The Mailu are great traders and sailors. As the island is to a large extent desolate and incapable of supporting its population of some 600 souls, the natives of Mailu Island are compelled to trade. Their expert seamanship and their fine vessels give these a great pull over the natives of other neighbouring coasts. The Island too is eminently adapted on account of its geographical position, as a great trading centre on the Southern coast. The Islanders are traders for they not only exchange their own goods for the things they want, but they also act as middlemen exchanging articles brought from the far east, as far as the Trobriands, and exchanging them to great advantage as far west as Aroma, where the native trades from Hood Bay, and even the Motuans met and carried westward their trading business, even to the far west limit of Papua. It is in July-August that the regular trading season begins, and in the present day times, when there is no possibility of raids, most of the able bodied men leave the village. The first expedition is generally made to Aroma, when they purchase betel nut etc. for pottery. On this expedition they fish along the reefs for the armlet shell (*Conus millepunctatus*), the reefs extending the whole way from Mailu to Aroma. Strange too they secure unworked armshells from the Aroma people, which are subsequently manufactured into armlets and other ornaments and these form the principal articles of trade with Aroma. During September and October they go to Lea to make sago and as they produce more than their wants, the surplus is sold to the Aroma people for small pigs and dogs. After the second expedition they sail during Nov-Dec eastward to Bonabona Isld, and further along the coast. There they acquire arm shells in return for the small pigs and dogs which they had obtained from Aroma. The best armshells are manufactured at the Trobriand Islands, the Mailu make armshells themselves, but it pays them to trade armshells from the far east to Aroma in the west owing to the difference of prices. The Mailu also understand some of the tricks in increasing the value of an armshell. The value of an armshell is estimated according to the position it occupies on a man's arm. The higher up it will go and the easier it will retain its position on a strong man's biceps, the more valuable it is, and to this end the Mailu frequently grind down the shells to make them slide further up the arm. About the beginning of January the trading expedition to Bonabona returned, after which the Mailu set out on their final expedition to Aroma. On this occasion armshells a number of which had been manufactured at home are exchanged for pigs. They are brought back, and usually at once used up for the feast.

Trading activities are now ended for the year, but as there is a big feast every year the trading is resumed each season, and is intimately connected with all the preparations for the feast, are interwoven with the preliminary festivities. It absorbs the whole social life of the Mailu for the better part of the year. The trading is essentially seasonal and regular, each expedition forming a step in a consecutive series of ceremonial transactions and industrial activities, making armshells, sago, pottery, and everything leading up to the final expedition that brought back the all important pig. (Diary C, 9-10 June 1921)

V.4489

V.4506   *Mailu women preparing vines as canoe lashings, Central Province. 7-11 June 1921.*

At the end of the trading season the Mailu canoes are refurbished. The work is a communal effort for which the canoe owner rewards the helpers with food. Here a group of women is preparing vines for securing the freeboard strakes and other parts of the canoe. They are working behind the inland row of houses.

V.4487 *Mailu men refurbishing two double-hulled canoes, Central Province. 7-11 June 1921.*

Hurley's return visit to Mailu was at the end of the trading season, when the large double-hulled canoes (*orou*) were being refurbished. The canoes were hauled on rollers up on to the beach, and the owners organised women to prepare new vines for lashings. Here the male helpers are replacing the lashings which secured the freeboard strakes to the hulls.

The dugouts are at the present made of the wood of the Moda, one of the tall tropical trees with buttressed trunks. Before the advent of the white, the logs which were secured from the mainland, on the banks of the Bairebo River, were excavated with stone implements, now steel is used exclusively. The log after excavation was provided with a fairly high gunwale, made of two large planks placed one on either side and two short ones at the end. The gunwale is lashed to the dugout with vine (*tsinare*). To make the gunwale watertight with the dugout the gap is caulked with soft bark of a tree (*kailsio*). The planks which close the canoe at either end (*birilsa*) are covered with a design suggestive of a face. The two canoes are joined together by ten horizontal poles passing through holes made in the four gunwales planks and strongly lashed to them (horizontal poles called Iado). The canoe has one mast and one sail (*deudeu*). (Diary C, 9-10 June 1921)

According to Saville (1926: 133-4), the carved splash-boards at each end of the hulls are known as *birisa* and the bark used for caulking is *kaiso*.

An almost identical photograph has been published by Saville (1926: opposite page 73). It was taken from the same position and shows the same canoes being repaired. It differs only in having several boys wearing loin-cloths of European fabric. Malinowski, in his Foreword to Saville's book, complimented Saville on his photographs. Some of this praise, perhaps, should be given to Hurley, who may have assisted Saville.

V.4487

V.4503   *Canoe sail at Mailu, Central Province. 7-11 June 1921.*

The sail is spread out in the street separating the two rows of houses. Saville (1926: 135) records that the sails were made from many strips of plaited plant fibres, made up by women in lengths of 4-6 metres and 30-40 centimetres wide. These were assembled by the men into the characteristic Mailu 'crab-claw' shaped sail.

The sail is constructed of matting made from freshwater reed. The crab-claw form of sail is produced by the convex straining of both spars and by the curved shaping of the upper rim of the sail. The ropes by which the sail is hoisted pass through a hole in the top of the mast and are made fast to an lado at the base of the mast. Before hoisting the rope is moistened with seawater to make it run easily. The gaff when hoisted comes to the top of the mast at about 2/3 of its length. Both boom and gaff are attached to the bottom of the mast. The ropes pass to the last rear lado of the Larimia. In moderately rough weather they scandalise the sail by folding the bottom apex of the triangular matting so that the top of the sail falls much lower. In very rough weather the sail is lowered, cast off from the boom and gaff, then they highstop the tesk of the sail, putting a short spar across its belly to spread it out. The crew consists of a minimum of six men. It takes three to attend to the sail, and during rough weather two to steer. (Diary C, 9-10 June 1921)

V.4492   *Man making fishing net on Mailu Island, Central Province. 7-11 June 1921.)*

The Mailu had a range of fish nets according to the kinds of fish being caught. The largest and heaviest nets were for catching leather-jackets and dugong. The kind of net shown here was made from fibre string from the aerial roots of pandanus (Saville 1926: 179). At the top (not visible) would be small, light wooden floats. The man is attaching small mollusc valves to the bottom to serve as weights. At the man's feet is a model of a double-hulled sailing canoe.

Hurley did not record observing this man at work; his only reference to fishing is about the use of fish poison in pools on the reef (Diary C, 7 June 1921).

V.4534 *Village scene at Boianai, Goodenough Bay, Milne Bay Province. 25 May 1921.*

Hurley visited Boianai at the end of his tour of Anglican mission stations. At the time the mission was under the care of Reverend Gill. Hurley's initial response to Gill and the manner in which he ran the station was favourable, but largely on account of Gill's amusing, but slightly bizarre, mechanical interests, and his emphasis on systematic efficiency. Gill had a flair for inventing labour-saving devices and had incorporated many in his house. Later reflection suggested to Hurley that the question remained whether the mission's work was really very effective or, indeed, desirable (Diary C, 3 June 1921).

    Hurley spent two nights, possibly three at Boianai. On 24 May he photographed the mission school and mission area in general. On the following day he spent the morning taking photographs in the village, and visited several other nearby villages in the afternoon. The records do not identify in which village this photograph was taken.

V.4553   *Man carrying a hafted stone axe at Mukawa village, Milne Bay Province. April-May 1921.*

Mukawa is situated on the north side of Cape Vogel. Hurley visited Mukawa twice in 1921, staying a total of four nights with the Anglican missionary Thomlinson, his wife and the schoolteacher, Ms Moneypenny. The Thomlinsons had been there nineteen years, during which time the villages were relocated from defensive positions on hill tops to beach-side locations. The mission itself remained on a hill.
    Hurley did not record any details of photographs taken at Mukawa. In the published version of this photograph, Hurley identified the man as "Waragi, the Stoic". According to Hurley's caption, Waragi was actually using the stone adze to make a canoe (Hurley 1924: 86).

V.4564 *Man working on a fish net, Komabun village, Wanigela, Collingwood Bay, Oro Province. 10-18 May 1921.*

The name Wanigela (or Wanigera) refers to an area of Collingwood Bay embracing three coastal villages and an Anglican mission station. The people of Komabun and nearby Rainu speak the Austronesian Ubir language. A closely related language, Oyan (Stephens 1974: 32), is spoken at nearby Oreresan. Hurley records that at the time of his visit, a non-Austronesian language, Onjob, was also spoken in Oreresan (Diary C, 11 May 1921). Hurley's information on this and other matters relating to the Wanigela villages was obtained from the Anglican missionary, Fisher, at Wanigela. Hurley spent eight nights at Wanigela but lost time through bad weather and a fever.

Although his diary entries for the Wanigela visit are extensive, they do not mention this scene. It was probably posed especially for Hurley, since the net has both floats and sinkers attached which would normally be done only when the net weaving was finished. The man holds a wooden shuttle with string wrapped around it. Hurley's only mention of fish net-making on the north coast relates to the Buna area (Diary B, 26 April 1921).

V.4564

V.4562   *Interior of a house at Wanigela, Collingwood Bay, Oro Province. 10-18 May 1921.*

The records do not mention in which of the Wanigela villages this photograph was taken, but attribute it to 11 May 1921. On that day the three villages near the mission station competed in a canoe race against the Anglican mission boat, *Whitkirk*. In the afternoon Hurley visited the villages and took photographs. The contents of the house are probably seen as they actually were; the man may have been posed. For the canoe race Hurley noted that the start was delayed while the participants decorated themselves; the ornaments worn by the man here may indicate that he had taken part in the race.

V.4574 *Man of Ubir village, Wanigela, Collingwood Bay, Oro Province. 10-18 May 1921.*

Hurley may have taken this photograph on 14 May when he spent the day photographing the mission church and "native studies". The man shown here is posed with a stone-headed club in the right hand. On his head is a cassowary feather band, and over his left shoulder he carries a boars' tusk face ornament. This frames the face and is held in place by gripping a cross-bar in the teeth.

Two days earlier Hurley witnessed a display of spear use:

During the afternoon a deaf and dumb male gave us a wonderful display of spear manoeuvres. Wearing a hornbill headdress and the strange mask (GIBIGIBI) which frames the face with an outline of boars tusks, and smearing his face with black, the wearer was one of the most ferocious objects I have ever looked at. His parrying, lunging and thrusting and footwork was a triumph of skill and alacrity. (Diary C, 12 May 1921)

This kind of face ornament is also shown on V.4653, taken at Wonari village at the northern end of Collingwood Bay.

V.4595 *Two male dancers at Awanen village, Collingwood Bay, Oro Province. 8 May 1921.*

While Hurley was visiting the Anglican mission on Naniu Island at the northern end of Collingwood Bay, he visited several mainland villages. At one of these, Awanen, a marriage ceremony was underway:

Many of the people were plenteously smeared and painted with raddle, decorating themselves with croton leaves and feathers, and one couple — a bridal pair — were saturated with coconut oil and arrayed with all their worldly ornaments and filth. This latter is made from a small chile like bean, the seeds of which are pounded, making a thick red paste. This red mixture is rubbed into the hair, giving it a bright red appearance repulsive to the eye and touch. The smearing of this red salve over the upper parts of the body and hair is very common, and when one is being lifted from a boat over the shallows to the shore, a white suit is invariably soiled beyond wear. If one touches a native in this part, portion of the native comes away in the fingers in the form of filth, so covered are these people with raddle, oil and soot from their fires. (Diary C, 8 May 1921)

   We found many of the village men had decorated themselves freely with red clay, lime, and polished their bodies by freely anointing with coconut oil. In their armlets pieces of the beautiful croton were stuck, giving to the natives the appearance of gaudily plumaged parrots. (Diary C 9 May 1921).

At nearby Wonari, Hurley saw other men wearing similar ornaments, including combs stuck into the hair behind the ears:

. . . .two large combs which they stick in the hair just behind the ears, (called IMIIT), and from which hang strings of beads and seeds. Also a stiff fringe of cassowary feathers trimmed with a uniform edge and worn across the head from ear to ear. (Diary C, 8 May 1921)

V.4595

V.4653 *Man holding a stone-headed club and wearing a face ornament, Wonari village, Collingwood Bay, Oro Province. 8 May 1921.*

Wonari was visited while Hurley was staying at the Anglican mission on Naniu Island at the northern end of Collingwood Bay. This man holds a stone-headed club similar to that held by the Ubir (Wanigela) man of V.4574. Around his face is the boars' tusk ornament which Hurley also saw at Wanigela.

V.4653

V.4614   *Binandere men on house verandah, Emo village, Dyke Ackland Bay, Oro Province. April-May 1921.*

North and west from Collingwood Bay Hurley visited many villages speaking dialects of the Binandere languages (sometimes loosely called Orokaiva). The following photographs from Emo, Eroro and Ambasi are from that area.

Much of Hurley's visit to Emo, where he stayed with the Anglican missionary, Elder, was devoted to photographing sago production and scenery. On 30 April he went through the village taking photographs:

The Emo village, although quite small, has all the characteristic studies of native life and work going on. It is a village of activity. Clay pots are being made and baked; canoes are building; the Tapa cloth makers are busy. Canoes come and go laden with produce, and the cries of ORO TAI! ORO TAI! sound throughout the village as some new arrival enters, or a heavily freighted canoe comes down stream. The old women are busy on their low verandahs making nets or preparing meals. From within the dark interiors comes the boom boom of an occasional drum and a wild chant. Babes swing in the shade of the verandahs slung in nets and bright eyed youngsters with mats of hair follow in my wake, to watch the "Dim-Dim" with his dim-dim picture maker. Pigs roam the village and wretched skeleton-like mongrels set up a chorus of wails, like lost souls. (Diary B, 30 April, 1921)

V.4614

V.4598 *Sago production at Emo village, Dyke Ackland Bay, Oro Province. 2-3 May, 1921.*

The main food of the Binandere is taro, but sago is eaten in times of taro shortages. The sago palms are commonly seen on river banks and in swampy areas of the Binandere territory, and Hurley took a series of photographs illustrating all stages of producing the edible starch.

The method of preparation throughout is similar, ingenious and interesting. The palm is suited for cutting after about seven years, the condition being best when the large panicle of stag-antler like flower is thrown up. The tree selected was one of a large clump, 70 feet in height. The palm after being felled, measured from base to where the great leaf fronds begin, 52 feet. The outer covering bark is split and prized off by pointed stakes. The pith like interior is pounded out by means of wooden mallets — an extremely slow and laborious method. Troughs for washing are made from the large leaves, being cunningly cut around the stem and carefully peeled off — in fact, all the apparatus for the final preparations is made from the palm itself. The pounded up pithy interior is carried to the washing arrangement which is erected on the bank of a stream or waterhole. This comprises an upper trough where the pith is washed (called BEO), and a strainer made from coconut fibre (called PUSISI). The pith is placed in this trough and water scooped up and poured in. It is thoroughly washed — together with the filthy hands in three changes of water — the water after passing through the pith is highly charged with starchy matter, — the true sago — this liquid passes through the strainer and then flows into a lower trough (INGI) which is sealed up. As soon as this trough is full operations are suspended for several hours to allow the starch to settle. The water is then drawn off and the sago remains. Darkness coming on precluded my further operations which I will continue tomorrow. To extract the sago from a large tree takes five men three days — half of this time is given up to making a noise. About 200 lbs of sago is obtained from a mature palm. We returned to the Mission Station feeling very tired and after tea — hornbill being the piece-de-resistance, I set about developing the splendid results. (Diary C, 2 May 1921)

We went upstream today to complete the operations of Sago making left over from yesterday. Our boys were already busy on the job and it needed no informer to announce that we were nearing the scene of work, for wild calls and songs echoed down the river a mile away. More pith had been treated, and the lower trough had settled sufficiently to allow of the water being drained off. Bad light seriously hampered my work, but by using the largest aperture I filmed the water being drained off and the subsequent operations. A residue closely resembling wet corn flour was left in the trough. This was scooped up and moulded in a cylindrical lump of some 50 lbs in weight. The stem of a leaf being used for moulding. The lumps were placed on green leaves, and a fire of dry sago leaves kindled on top. The fierce heat cooks the outside of the mass, making it portable and protecting it against decay by the exclusion of air. I am told the wet sago keeps well in this condition for three weeks, but it is invariably eaten before it has opportunity of going bad. The bundles are then tied up in leaf and slung from the house rafters. The process though highly wasteful is extremely ingenious, all the appurtenances and plant being manufactured from the sago palm itself, except the strainer, which is cut from the coconut palm. (Diary C, 3 May 1921)

V.4642   *Binandere man chewing betel nut at Eroro village, near Oro Bay, Oro province. 29 April 1921.*

While Hurley was taking photographs at Beiama village on Oro Bay, a group of people from nearby Eroro came to ask him to film and take photographs of dancing in their village. Hurley went immediately and found several hundred people dressed and ready to dance. In addition to the dancers, he took several posed photographs of individuals. This man, about to lick his lime spatula, is wearing a hornbill headdress (*peremo*) and a double boars' tusk neck pendant (*hono*) which traditionally would signify that he has killed an enemy (Williams 1930: 39-40, 178-9). He is holding a gourd lime container (*okigi*) and a wooden spatula (*ota*). Lime was made by burning sea shells, crushing them and then slaking them with water in a banana leaf (Williams 1930: 65-6).

V.4656   *Binandere woman, Ambasi village, Oro Province. 18-23 April 1921.*

Hurley described this woman in his annotation of the photograph simply as "a rich heiress with her 'jewellery', Ambasi, Buna Bay". His diaries do not explain why she was so heavily ornamented, though he commented that

The natives wear a great display of ornaments around their necks, dogs' teeth, shells, boars' tusk etc., and strings of "white-man's" beads. Their hair is matted with coconut oil and dirt and finishes off at the back in a teasle of yarns like the plaited fringe on the end of a travelling rug. (Diary B, 19 April 1921)

This woman wears also ear ornaments of shell discs (*dende*) and arm rings of shell (*samemi*) and coconut shell (*siha*). Williams (1930: plate xxvi b) illustrates three girls wearing similar neck and arm ornaments after their initiation.

V.4656

V.4662 *Man lashing the platform on a canoe, Ambasi village, Oro Province. 18-23 April 1921.*

V.4663 *Two Binandere parents in mourning, Ambasi village, Oro Province. 19-20 April 1921.*

Hurley does not record the details of V.4662 in his diaries.

Hurley's visit to Ambasi coincided with the mourning for the death of a small child. His annotation for this photograph describes the subject as "Parents mourning loss of a child", possibly the one referred to in his diary.

Passing by one of the huts, a serenade of howls and wails issued and on enquiring the whyfor, was told they were professional mourners bewailing the death of a very young infant. The cries were of "New Guinea sadness" — they were merely exorcising evil spirits, of which the people here dwell in eternal shivers. (Diary B, 19 April 1921)

The woman has covered her head and upper body with white clay, the man has treated only his hair in this fashion.

V.4662

V.4663

75

V.4672   *Decorated girls and widow, Ambasi village, Oro Province. 18-23 April 1921.*

Hurley does not specifically refer to this group, which was probably posed especially for him. The girls are wearing ornaments similar to the initiates illustrated by Williams (1930: plate xxvi b) but may have been dressed this way for the photograph. The woman seated on the ground is a widow in mourning. She is covered with white clay, her hair has been cut short, and she wears a mourning dress of the seeds of Job's tears (*Coix lacrimae*).

   Hurley observed a widow at Koira village inland from Ambasi on the Opi River (Hurley 1924: 93):

She was smothered from head to foot with white mud. I learned that she was a widow and in mourning for the recent death of her husband. The hair had been clipped short and there she sat on the verandah of her small hut, the picture of abject misery, loneliness and hideousness. I am told the custom till recently was — that the widow had to remain indoors until a great feast was given to the spirit of the departed. This meant waiting until a prolific period and frequently the wretched creature might remain indoors for over a year. During this time she works a bodice-like jacket of small shells, which she dons when she is free and wears in public. (Diary B, 20 April 1921)

V.4637 *Two policemen from Buna village, Oro Province, on patrol with Hurley to Ononge, Central Province. July 1921.*

Following discussions with the Lieutenant-Governor, J.H.P. Murray, Hurley decided to visit the Mafulu area inland from Hall Sound at the end of his first expedition (Diary C, 16 and 20 June 1921). While en route to Kikori, Hurley visited Kairuku Island to make arrangements for the patrol with the Assistant Resident Magistrate, Mr W.R. Humphries. On his return from Kikori, Hurley found that Father Bach of the Sacred Heart Mission was planning a tour of mission stations in the area south and east of Mafulu as far as Ononge. Hurley took the opportunity to accompany Father Bach, and extended his stay in Papua by three weeks.

Until this point, his visit had been coastally-oriented, dictated as much by the coastal locations of the Anglican mission stations as by the difficulties of inland patrols.

Hurley was accompanied by two policemen of the Papua Armed Constabulary recruited from Buna village, Oro Province, and based on Kairuku Island. Humphries seconded them to Hurley to assist him with the supervision of his line of 30 carriers. Humphries' own experiences patrolling in the mountains had shown him the reluctance of coastal carriers to travel far from their home villages, while the hostility displayed towards Humphries by the various mountain peoples on previous patrols probably made him concerned for Hurley's safety. However, Hurley was travelling with missionaries to mission stations and at no point of the patrol was any violence, threatened or actual, recorded in Hurley's diaries.

The corporal (left) was instructed by Humphries to arrest a suspected murderer at Fane village, inland from Dilava. The corporal sought Hurley's assistance but Hurley refused, tersely noting in his diary:

I told the corporal I was no punitive expedition and to forget the magistrate's order. (Diary D, 14 July 1921)

No arrest was made.

V.4251 *Dilava Roman Catholic Mission, Central Province. 9-10 July 1921.*

V.4338 *Road building by missionaries inland from Hall Sound, Central Province. July 1921.*

Two-and-a-half days' walk inland from Hall Sound, Hurley and Father Bach reached Dilava Mission, one of a group of stations set up by the Sacred Heart Mission to serve the Kuni and Fuyuge speakers of the Goilala language family on the east side of the Angabunga River. Here they were entertained by Father Chabot and the brothers for two nights. Hurley, on his first patrol into the mountainous interior of Papua, took advantage of the rest day to record photographically the spectacular scenery.

> . . . all of a sudden as we topped the summit, the most wonderful panorama of mountain scenery burst upon us. On a cleared area stood the mission station, and over the lip of the clearing, falling to an abysmal gully, the prospect of a maze of noble peaks topped by scudding mists provided a prospect worthy of a world tour to witness. (Diary D, 9 July 1921)
> . . . All the timber for the Station has been cut from the nearby ridges, shaped and planed, the galvanised roofing alone has been carried from Yule Island. The church is an ample structure some 70 feet x 40 and is walled and lined with planed wood. The altars and cabinets, seating and furniture has all been made locally, the products of Brother Jules mill. . . . .It is a miniature cathedral set amidst wild and rugged surroundings. The Station is built on the crest of a small spur which juts out like a grand lookout over a deep valley encircled by mighty ranges. The residence where the priests and brothers reside is equally as well constructed.. . . (Diary D, 10 July 1921)

Many stretches of Hurley's patrol into the mountains of the Goilala speakers were eased by roads built by the Fathers of the Sacred Heart Mission, many of whom used horses for moving between the villages under their care. The roads were intended, however, for wheeled vehicles, the first of which arrived after Hurley's visit. According to J.H.P. Murray, Lieutenant-Governor of Papua, by 1921 the missionaries had supervised the construction of 175 kilometres of road between Aropokina on the coast and Ononge Mission, though not all sections were easily traversed on account of landslides and difficulties of maintenance under heavy tropical rains. Of the road construction generally, Hurley recorded:

> The road has been entirely constructed by the Sacred Heart Mission partly subsidised by the administration, in the shape of providing tools, and payment of natives. The surveying has been done entirely by the fathers and their time given without recompense. (Diary D, 7 July 1921)

The precise location and date of this photograph is uncertain. The museum's Photography Register ascribes its location to 'near Ononge', but this is unlikely since Hurley describes the roads in the Ononge area as completed. It could be the Dilava — Deva Deva section which was being built under the direction of Father Eschlimann at the time of Hurley's visit:

> . . . .he is making a new road between Dilava and Deva Deva which will dispense with the great descent of over 1000 feet and the 1½ hours rise to 1500 feet on the opposite ridge. . . . .Fine work he is doing, hewing a track from the huge forest trees and grading a pathway on the sides of ridges. He has some 60 boys engaged, their payment being in tobacco, salt, axes or knives and similar articles. His little camp is comfortably situated in a small clearing surrounded by giant forest trees and hemmed in by high ranges. (Diary D, 11 July 1921)

The identities of the two missionaries are uncertain, though they are probably Fathers Eschlimann and Bach. Hurley's admiration for the missionaries' efforts is evident from his comments on the road to Ononge from Mount Tafa:

> . . . .from the Tafa to Ononge the track is wonderful. It ceases to be a mere track and almost becomes a road. The track has been carried around high mountain contours, so as to avoid mountain torrents and is superbly graded. It follows around bluff mountains, cut on the edge of gorges, even slightly and gradually descending for Ononge is at least 2,000 feet below the Tafa road which is 8,000 feet above sea level. As one descends into the valley, the trees and foliage become more luxuriant than that which grows on the bleak heights of the Tafa. The road, kept clear and free from all vegetation and overgrowth, is more like a road through a beautiful natural garden than a way into the heart of New Guinea. (Diary D, 16 July 1921)

V.4251

V.4338

81

V.4270 *Man of Dilava village, Central Province. 29 July 1921.*

Dilava village is situated south and east of the middle reaches of the Angabunga River, where the Austronesian Kuni language is spoken. Hurley visited Dilava on both the outward and return journeys to Ononge, staying at the mission station. On the outward journey, he noted:

Dilava is 700 feet below me. I went down to it this morning a slippery walk down a tumbling, native track, through grasses, bamboos and thickets. . . . The people themselves are a healthy looking assemblage in spite of the damp mists, crude in their ways and extremely primitive. The women wear most of their clothes around their neck in the form of necklets of boar's tusks and dog's teeth, the latter are also plaited in the hair. They are comely to look upon, well proportioned and free from the hideous skin diseases and yaws which are the characteristic of coastal villages. They wear for garments a small piece of fibre which scarcely covers the private part — the same for the men, and yet they do not appear immodest nor are they immoral. (Diary D, 10 July 1921)

This man is described in the museum Photography Register as a "Bridegroom of Dilava Village, hair in wooden cylinders". The photograph was taken on the return journey from Ononge. As Hurley was approaching Dilava he was met on the track by a carrier from the coast bringing him a new supply of photographic plates and news of the birth of his third child. At Dilava he encountered Mr W. Baker, a temporary Patrol Officer from Kairuku, on his way to patrol the country beyond Ononge. In his Annual Report for 1920-21 to the Australian Parliament, the Lieutenant-Governor, J.H.P. Murray, records the patrol as being under Patrol Officer C.A. Leonard (Australia 1922: 12). Murray himself had visited the area, and Ononge specifically, in 1912.

V.4271 *Village Constable at Dilava village, Central Province. 9-29 July 1921.*

Hurley visited Dilava on both the outward and return journey to Ononge. His diary does not record when this photo was taken, nor the identity of the constable.

Village constables were unarmed government appointees who performed police duties in their villages and provided advice and information to the magistrate responsible for their areas. This system, introduced in 1890 by Sir William MacGregor, supplemented the more formal Armed Constabulary who were based at government stations.

The Photography Register of the Australian Museum identifies this constable as "probably a migrant from Mekeo". Dilava is in the Kuni language area, with the Mekeo to the south and west. Why a Mekeo man should have been living in Dilava with the Village Constable's position, is not clear.

V.4332 *Sacred Heart Mission Station at Ononge, Central Province. 16-21 July 1921.*

Ononge Mission Station, founded in 1913 by Father Dubuy, was reached after a wet night's camp in moss forest at about 2,300 metres altitude. Father Bach went ahead, leaving Hurley to photograph orchids in the moss forest. Although weary after an eight-and-a-half hour walk carrying his camera equipment, Hurley preferred to walk the last few kilometres to Ononge, rather than ride on a horse sent for him by Father Dubuy.

The building in the background was a new residence for Father Dubuy and his colleagues. Sawn timbers for this structure came from a water-powered sawmill. The small church on the right was a temporary building following the burning down of the original structure. A photograph of the Station taken in about 1940 shows a large new church and other buildings (Dupeyrat 1954: opposite page 177).

Two days before reaching Ononge, Hurley reflected on the origin of the extensive grasslands near Fane village, and later remarked on the grasslands near Ononge. At Fane he recorded:

The scenery is more open, for in place of the dense gloom of the jungles the landscape opens up into vast grassy undulations, here and there patched by forest glades and jungles. These grassy patches no doubt are due to the natives having from time to time made clearings for their gardens. And, as only one crop is planted, and after its reaping the area is allowed to lie fallow, another area is felled. So this has continued with the result that the country looks like grassland areas. Strange too that when the trees are cut down they don't appear to throw up shoots or suckers, but rapidly decay. (Diary D, 14 July 1921)

At Evese village, near Ononge, Hurley observed that:

After a garden is made and the fruits of the soil reaped, the people burn off another site and allow the previous one to lay fallow. Perhaps ten years might elapse before the old garden site is dug again. This accounts for the extensive cleared and grassy areas noticeable throughout the valley. (Diary D, 20 July 1921)

V.4321 *House in Ononge area, Central Province. 20-21 July 1921.*

This photograph was probably taken in Evese village near Ononge. Hurley visited Evese on 20 July 1921, and noted in his diary:

The houses are small pyramidal wedge shaped cots thatched with pandanus palm leaves and built 3 to 4 feet above the ground on piles. They are situated on the crest of knolls which rise from the innumerable low scarps which undulate down to the Vanapa river. The houses are small and built detached around the perimeter of a small cleared area. They are not protected, in their exposed situations, which points to a very moderate climate . . . The old men were duly posed and photographed, together with their houses and whatever presented, though their arts and crafts are nil and they do little beyond making nets for catching wild pigs. (Diary D, 20 July 1921)

Hurley revisited Evese on 21 July 1921, to make sound recordings of village songs about the rivers, birds, flowers and daily life. The phonograph had been carried by two men from the coast and this was the first occasion Hurley used it on the patrol. Although Hurley and Father Bach had 30 carriers and the patrol was not a major one by Papuan standards, the use of carriers to transport the phonograph and photographic equipment meant a reduction in the quantity of food that they could carry. The diaries record on several occasions during this patrol how the party was short of food even though they were able to buy some local produce and on many nights Hurley and Bach were guests at mission stations.

V.4355 *Two men of Mondo village, Central Province. 22 July 1921.*

Hurley passed through Mondo village twice on his patrol to Ononge; this photograph was taken on the second visit. The Mondo people, situated in the mountains between the headwaters of the Angabunga and Vanapa rivers, speak a non-Austronesian language of the Goilalan family.

Mondo, together with Belavista and Fane, is described as an 'outstation' of Popole Mission under the care of Father Dontenwill at Popole. Hurley described them as follows:

All these stations are cosy little hamlets, with their church and little cottages, the woods being the product of Father Fastre's mill. (Diary D, 14 July, 1921)

On their return visit to Mondo, they found that both the church and house had been burnt down. Father Dontenwill suspected arson, a distinct possibility since the Ononge church had also recently been destroyed by fire (Hurley 1924: 171). At nearby Belavista, Hurley described the mountain people as:

. . . .diminutive in stature, being scarcely over 5 feet 7 inches, though well proportioned and robust. They wear a long bone through the septum of the nose and strange decorations, generally the eye teeth of dogs, dangling from the conch of the ear. These teeth are also plaited into the hair, all over the head, and are the mountain currency. Necklets of dogs' teeth are also worn, and a small flat shell breastplate, adorned in the centre with tortoise shell carved to apparently imitate a cogwheel from an alarm clock. Recently at Deva Deva I observed a village policeman wearing a real wheel for an earring, and this has evidently been the model for the designs. The body is entirely bare with the exception of a small fibre triangle just — almost covering the private parts. (Diary D, 14 July 1921)

The identity of these two men is not known. Their appearance generally does not match that given in Hurley's description above and it is not clear why this should be so. The description was recorded during preparations for a feast at Belavista, when the people may have been especially ornamented. The Deva Deva village constable referred to in the above diary extract appears on negative V.4281 (not reproduced in this volume).

V.4369 *Chief's house at Inawaia village, Central Province. 2-4 August 1921.*

V.4370 *Woman's house at Inawaia village, Central Province. 2-4 August 1921.*

At the end of his patrol to Ononge, Hurley spent three nights in the Mekeo village of Inawaia with Father Bronchier at the Sacred Heart Mission Station. The Mekeo are an Austronesian language speaking group who are cut off from direct access to the coast by the Roro people. The Mekeo are divided into two main groups, or tribes. Inawaia belongs to the Ve'e tribe which is mostly located east of the Angabunga River. Inawaia itself is close to the border with the Roro. Traditionally each sub-clan or alliance within the Mekeo has two hereditary chiefs for civilian and military affairs, with the civilian chief having a substitute or second-in-command. To which chief the house shown here belonged, is not known.

In strict tribal law the village huts are occupied by the women, children and the girls, the chief of the family takes up his residence with his sons in another hut behind that of the women. Bachelors and widowers dwell in a large house by themselves . . . (Diary D, 2 August 1921)

Mekeo villages are arranged with the houses in rows around a rectangular open area. Only the chiefs' houses may face this area; the other houses face away from it. The chiefs' houses, and those of their assistants, have elaborate roof designs and special hangings (*ipaipa*) on their sides and ends (Hau'ofa 1971: 154, 162).

Seligmann (1910: plates 42, 44, 45) illustrates several Mekeo houses, some of quite distinctive design.

Hurley's visit to Inawaia coincided with preparations for a feast and a singing competition between clans of Inawaia and neighbouring villages. The feast comprised mainly taro and bananas, here piled on the platform outside a woman's house, cooked in earthenware pots acquired from the coastal Roro people.

At present a feast is being given by one clan of the village to another, and all the women are busy carrying in immense piles of Bananas and Taro for the event. The feast is only a small one and probably the paying back, to the invited guests, of a similar feast given by the now guests to the present hosts in some by-gone time. (Diary D, 3 August 1921)

Though the guests are invited from the neighbouring clan it plays no active part in the feast giving or making. All day women have been busy collecting food and preparing foodstuffs for the event. All the men appear to be doing towards the affair is to spend the day painting their faces and adorning their hair . . . Girls from the houses brought large earthen bowls of cooked Taro, potatoes, bananas, etc. for food and the singers took shifts eating it. (Diary D, 3 August 1921)

V.4369

V.4370

93

V.4384 & V.4381   *Singing contest at Inawaia village, Central Province. 4 August 1921.*

Mekeo chiefs construct club houses or *ufu* for the male members of their subclan. The *ufu* is the focal point of male clan activities, and the place where visiting chiefs are entertained. Each *ufu* usually has a carved post supporting the thatched overhang of the roof at its entrance (Seligmann 1910: 330-4), in front of which the *pikei* singing contest takes place.

Mekeo clans and villages engage in singing contests (*pikei*) in which one group tries to out-sing and thus humiliate the other. The contests last several days, with half of each side singing at any one time while the other half rests. Hurley's visit to Inawaia coincided with a contest between a clan of Inawaia and one from several neighbouring villages, which began on 3 August and was still going on when Hurley left on 4 August.

In *Pearls and Savages* (P.129) Hurley published a photograph of the contest titled 'A Native Eistedfodd at Mekeo' which is almost identical to V.4384. The glass plate negative of the *Pearls and Savages* photograph is held by the National Library of Australia.

In the afternoon the guests began to put in an appearance, their bodies smeared with a mixture of ochre and coconut oil, wearing all their available ornaments and their faces painted with grotesque patterns. After dark the singing began, and I went down to the village to see what was going on. The painted guests and hosts were seated in front of the village chief's UFU (Club House). The girls on one side and the men on the other, a camp fire between them. The leader of the song began a weird monotonous rambling chant, the melody confined to three notes, and this was repeated for hours. The words were not of their language and I doubt if any, excepting the old men, really understood them. (Diary D, 3 August 1921)

I was up early with the camera and with Father Bronchier's assistance took pictures of the various singers — the chant still going strong. When the sun rose so as to be too hot to sing in their previous station, the crowd moved off towards a tree and continued again. As some tired they went off to sleep and the waking sleepers carried on.

At 4 pm the painted singers and guests began to come from the circumjacent villages, and singing began at 4.30 pm — when the sun had fallen behind the palms . . . The women seated themselves on the ground at a small distance from the men's Club House, and the men seated on the platform in front of it. A leader of the song was selected and he opened with a chant-like dirge. The song would not be of more than four to five bars, and the words seemed to be equivalent to our Tra-la-la. Father Bronchier who stood by me and who is thoroughly acquainted with the language said that even when words are used they may not know the meaning, or else if they do the words are as simple as our nursery rhymes. (Diary D, 4 August 1921)

When we packed up our "traps" and left Inawaia the same few bars had impressed themselves indelibly on my memory. (Diary D, 4 August 1921)

V.4384

V.4381

V.4374　*Two singers from the singing contest at Inawaia Village, Central Province. 4 August 1921.*

An important element of the *pikei* singing contest among the Mekeo is body decoration. According to Humphries (1923: 226), lack of such decoration would be unlucky and would lead to defeat. Humphries records how a group of people from Inawaia was insulted while passing through Veifa'a village by being challenged to a *pikei* when they did not have their body ornaments. The Inawaia people had to decline the challenge and suffered loss of face. For the *pikei* witnessed by Hurley:

The men were decorated with fine tattoo like paintings over the face, each being different. The hair was given great attention and decorated with feathers. In the noses a long narrow pencil — pointed at either end and ground from the clam shell seven inches long were worn. (Diary D, 4 August 1921)

According to Seligmann (1910: 320ff), each clan has distinctive body ornaments, *kangakanga*, which serve to identify the clan. These *kangakanga* are usually named after a plant or small animal. For some clans the *kangakanga* may not be eaten, but parts of the animal or plant are used in the body decorations. For Inawaia, Seligmann's information is incomplete and he lists only the cockerel *(oölo)* (Seligmann: 1910: 372).

V.4376 *Old man of Inawaia Village, Central Province. 4 August, 1921.*

Most of Hurley's photographs taken in Inawaia were directed towards the houses, feast and *pikei* singing contest. The older people seem not to have participated in the contest, being satisfied to watch the proceedings from the side. This man, carrying a bamboo smoking pipe and wearing a length of bamboo in his earlobe, may be watching the *pikei*.

The small boys and girls of the village grouped around them (the singers) in a crowd whilst the other village people just looked on, seeming to regard little the performance . . . The rest of the village people took no heed of the singing; they evidently having tired of it and the small boys now and then chimed in, in mocking strains. Yet the tireless singers sang on as if they had an ardent duty to perform. (Diary D, 4 August 1921)

V.5001 *The* Eureka *on Lake Murray, Western Province. 15-24 November 1922.*

Lake Murray is the largest lake in Papua New Guinea, between the Fly and Strickland rivers. At the time of Hurley's visit the area was regarded as unexplored, though explorers and administration staff had visited more remote areas along the Fly and its headwaters, and the Strickland. The lake was first visited by an administration patrol in 1913, and was named after the Lieutenant-Governor, J.H.P. Murray. In 1914 Murray himself visited the lake and in his Annual Report to the Australian government provided a brief description of it and its inhabitants (Australia 1914: 18-22).

Hurley's original plan was to take his vessel, the *Eureka,* up to Lake Murray with the Assistant Government Anthropologist, F.E. Williams. There they would rendezvous with the Lieutenant-Governor, and the Curtiss 'Seagull' flown by Lang and Hill. He arrived too late to meet up with Murray, and without Williams or the plane.

Murray, it later transpired, had visited only that part of the lake where it joined the Herbert River. While Hurley's publicity was rather overstated (e.g. in *The Sun* of 6, 7 and 8 February 1923, and Hurley 1924: 367ff), he appears to have explored more parts of the lake than his predecessors and may have made first contact with one group of people.

The *Eureka* entered Lake Murray on 15 November and although they saw a canoe in the distance and visited a deserted longhouse, a week passed before they had any contact with the people. The *Eureka* was fitted with its wireless aerial for communicating with Port Moresby and Thursday Island. McCulloch made contact with Thursday Island only once while on Lake Murray, since atmospheric conditions severely affected transmission.

V.4974 *Human skull on a stake on the track leading to a longhouse, Lake Murray, Western Province. 16 November 1922?*

The *Eureka* entered Lake Murray on 15 November. Hurley records seeing a canoe in the distance and a deserted longhouse. On 16 November Hurley went ashore with McCulloch and four of his boat crew, "all strongly armed with rifles and revolvers". As they approached the longhouse,

. . . . before we reached the dubu (longhouse) the track was "closed" by a skull on a pole and arrows. These we removed and replaced with emblems of peace. A broken bough, strings of beads, red calico, and a number of benzine tins for these people are destitute of cooking utensils beyond sections of bamboo . . . . (Diary 2, 16 November 1922)

Inside the longhouse Hurley

. . . secured a particularly fine specimen of a human head. This gruesome object had the human skin stuffed and fancifully decorated. I am told these stuffed heads are greatly valued and are looked upon as the emblems of a warrior, power and wealth. The head and neck is severed from the body, so that the neck may be retained as long as possible. The skin is split up the back and the fleshy parts extracted. I am uncertain as to whether the skull is utilised in the final stuffing, or whether clay is simply used as a cast over which the skin is strained. I am inclined to the former. The skull and skin is smoked for preservation and the hair is all removed. The shape is secured by stuffing with clay and grass and the skin is finally brought together at the back by lacing it together. The face is distorted as illustrated in No. 1 being lengthened considerably. A large ball of clay is placed in the mouth which is strained excessively open. The eye sockets are filled with clay and the external skin is decorated with red and yellow ochre. (Diary 2, 17 November 1922)

Several of these heads are shown in V.4986. The National Library of Australia holds a glass plate of this skull taken from a slightly different angle (Hurley 1924: 19).

V.4974

103

V.4986 *Allan McCulloch with Lake Murray artefacts and skulls in the grounds of the museum, Port Moresby, National Capital District. 16-17 January 1923.*

On their return to Port Moresby at the end of the second expedition, Hurley and McCulloch found that a complaint alleging unethical collecting methods had been laid against them by the Resident Magistrate on Daru (see V.4389, V.5207). All of their collections were impounded, pending an inquiry, and were taken to the "local museum" in Port Moresby (Diary 4, 16 January 1923). This photograph was apparently taken on the day after the confiscation.

The museum in Port Moresby was under the control of the Commissioner for Native Affairs. It was a small building and in 1915 the Lieutenant-Governor arranged for the reserve collections to be stored at the Australian Museum in Sydney where, he felt, conditions were better suited to the preservation of the artefacts and there was experienced staff. Several thousand artefacts were shipped to Sydney to be incorporated into what became known as the "official Papuan Collection". In 1934 the collection was transferred to the custody of the Australian government, being housed in the Institute of Anatomy, Canberra. The complaint against Hurley and McCulloch was eventually resolved by the confiscation and return to Kaimari in the Purari delta of several bull-roarers and a *kwoi* board; nothing was returned to Lake Murray. In his diary Hurley noted that the practices adopted by McCulloch and himself on Lake Murray were exactly those used by the Lieutenant-Governor's party which visited the lake several weeks before Hurley (Diary 4, 16 January 1923). Hurley believed that his own actions were more honourable, for he left more valuable gifts in exchange for artefacts than did Murray.

On 17 January the Official Secretary, James Baldie, wrote to Hurley citing the "Papuan Antiquities Ordinance, 1913" under which "curios (not on the free list) must be offered to the Commissioner for Native Affairs and, if he desires to purchase them for the Papuan Collection, a reasonable price must be paid" (letter in Diary 4, 17 January 1923). Baldie was unaware, or chose to ignore, that McCulloch had sent on the previous day to Staniforth Smith, who was acting as Administrator in the Lieutenant-Governor's absence, a copy of a letter to the Resident Magistrate, Daru, which indicates a prior agreement with the administration. McCulloch was under the impression that the collections should be sent direct to Sydney and a list subsequently would be sent to Baldie by the Director of the Australian Museum. Baldie could then advise which artefacts should be transferred to the Papuan Collection held in storage in Sydney.

It is of interest that none of the artefacts shown in this photograph has an obvious identification tag on it. This raises a question about the accuracy of locality attributions subsequently assigned to artefacts registered in the Australian Museum.

V.4986

105

V.5021 *Man of Lake Murray, Western Province. 23 November 1922.*

In the published caption to this portrait Hurley identifies the man as "Hamoji, the Chief", and includes another view of him as the Frontispiece. Nowhere in Hurley's diary is the name of any Lake Murray person recorded, so it is not clear where and when the name was obtained. The *Pearls and Savages* version of this photograph has been treated to remove the background scenery of the shore of Lake Murray.

In common with other men of Lake Murray, this man's hair is plaited. Many of Hurley's photographs show that plaiting or rolling of the hair in 'dreadlocks' was formerly more common in parts of Papua than has hitherto been realised. The front part of the scalp has been shaved, accentuating the plaits. According to Hurley (1924: 400), the natural length of the plaits has been increased by adding lengths of plant fibre.

This photograph was probably taken from or on the deck of the *Eureka* on 23 November 1922, when several canoes visited the ship and Hurley persuaded at least one man to come aboard to have his photograph taken (see V.5015).

V.5021

V.5026   *Two Lake Murray men visiting the* Eureka, *Western Province. 22-23 November 1922.*

The visit of Lake Murray men to the *Eureka* on 22 November 1922 led to a lively trade between the Lake Murray people and Hurley and McCulloch, and established a friendly relationship between them.

Matches, the taste of sugar and salt alike astonished and pleased them, but what they clamoured for was the empty tins, which we had saved for the purpose, and empty oil and benzine tins. These primitive folk are entirely destitute of utensils of any description beyond bamboo, and a few water baskets made by folding the leaf sheath of the Goru palm. For a few tins we purchased a bundle of arrows, while the same currency bought paddles, stone clubs, etc. They were also very anxious to secure axes and knives, which we exchanged, securing great value for our tools. (Diary 2, 22 November 1922)

Some of these men returned the following day, and further trading took place:

Jam tins and milk tins bought bundles of arrows and paddles and other things. What we would cast away to them was of inestimable value. We had saved all our empties for this purpose so our trading was profitable. The tin of tomatoes, with its two-penny worth of fruit and threepenny tin (that cost 2/-) proved after all a profitable investment. Often I had ranted over the iniquitous robbery of paying 2/- for a tin of tomatoes worth 2d. Now the empty tins bought for us what was worth pounds! (Diary 2, 23 November 1922)

In *Pearls and Savages* Hurley published a photograph of McCulloch "bartering empty tomato cans for skulls and arrows . . . ." (Hurley 1924: 381).

After the trading and photography, the canoes and the *Eureka* went to the village. Seeing that the women and children were not present and suspecting danger, Hurley and McCulloch did not land. The Lake Murray men started dancing and playing their drums, and McCulloch made a recording of the music. Hurley was surprised to find that the benzine tins which he had traded, thinking that they would make good containers for cooking, were in fact appreciated as substitute drums.

V.5015 *Allan McCulloch showing a photograph to a man on Lake Murray. 23 November 1922.*

Hurley's party finally made contact, on 22 November, with people from Dukoif village (originally recorded in his diary as Segaro village). On the next day Hurley took the *Eureka* some distance from Dukoif towards the point where they had entered the lake. In the morning several canoes visited the ship, including people seen on the previous day. He persuaded one of the men to go on board the *Eureka* and have his photograph taken:

I lost no time in getting busy with my cameras, and made the limit of my opportunities. We rigged up blanket for a background, and induced, after great coaxing and persuasion, one to come aboard and "pose". I don't blame the poor chap appearing nervously brave and all the time wanting to peer round to see what was going on behind the blanket. I forgot in my desires that this blanket would cause alarm. I can imagine our own feelings if a barrier were placed behind us in a village, and we were coaxed to sit in front of it whilst suspicious characters with deadly weapons were moving about behind the screen. Then I found it well nigh impossible for him to keep still, he was unusually fidgety and not at all an easy subject. Presently the sitter noticed his reflection in the lens, this again required many sambios and explanations to reassure him. Eventually McCulloch brought out a few paper prints and I also let the native view his fellows through the reflex camera. (Diary 2, 23 November 1922)

Hurley's party used the word "sambio" as a peaceful signal, though McCulloch's brief vocabulary recorded in Hurley's diary under 23 November 1922, shows it to mean "come".

V.5015

V.4943 *Three longhouses at Adulu village, near the mouth of the Fly River, Western Province. 5 December 1922.*

Three nights were spent at Adulu village on the return from Lake Murray. After several days travelling down the Strickland and Fly rivers without visiting any settlements, Hurley was ready to continue photographing and purchasing artefacts.

Eventually we reached ADURU and a number of men came out in canoes to trade bananas. After lunch McCulloch and I and several natives went ashore. We were greatly pleased to find the people tractable and well disposed. The Hebraic cast was still present and the hair worn in small stiff curls which pended like a very coarse mop. They were a jovial crowd and displayed hospitality, so that I had no fear for our safety. The village which comprised three large and long houses, was pictorially situated on the banks of a creek just off the main stream. A number of fine canoes of great proportions were moored in the creek several decorated with high prows, and each capable of carrying up to 15 men. I was astonished to find good order and comparative cleanliness in the village and the comparative scarcity of mud. The houses were built upon piles, remarkably well constructed and approached by rather a pretentious series of banistered steps. The largest of the houses measured 195 feet long and some 30 feet wide. (Diary 2, 2 December 1922)

Hurley later took movie film of the canoes being towed by the *Eureka* and was impressed by them:

After securing the film we cast off the canoes, and had ample opportunities of observing their method of handling and propelling their vessels. These canoes are unexcelled throughout the Territory for the excellence of their workmanship, being up to 50 feet long and beautifully excavated. The outrigger is secured on to the dugout proper by two slender distance pieces, or poles, which are fastened to the outrigger by a number of slender struts. These latter are so arranged as to prevent movement laterally or longitudinally. The whole arrangement is light and possessed of great strength. The vessel might be considered graceful and elegant. The paddlers up to 15 for a 50 feet vessel sit on small cane cross pieces which are bound into the top sides of the canoe. The vessel, once it is under way, (which is done by sweeping, broad strokes) is kept in motion by short rapid strokes. The method of propulsion evidently being more efficient in the swift running current than long broad sweeps. It is worthy of note that these canoes can maintain readily the speed of our vessel against the current, and in spurts readily pass us. (We are capable of making a speed of six knots.) (Diary 2, 4 December 1922)

While at Adulu, McCulloch succeeded in sending a wireless message for the first time in three weeks, having been hindered by atmospheric interference. This time, however, he had the noise of excited villagers as a background:

When we managed to explain to the natives that we required absolute silence, they readily did their best, and I must say McCulloch had little to complain of. The people are some of the finest that I have yet met in Papua, as regards physique, looks and tractability. They are a jovial crowd, making fun of the slightest antic, and we keep them thoroughly amused, for in their ideas most of the things we do are strange and amusing, just as we regard them. As I make this entry three canoe loads are around the vessel, making a personnel of some 60. It is very difficult to keep them quiet. (Diary 2, 4 December 1922)

V.4943

V.4946 *Interior of longhouse at Adulu village, near the mouth of the Fly River, Western Province. 2-5 December 1922.*

Hurley and McCulloch visited Adulu just as a mortuary feast was being prepared. The women were still in their mourning dress, and large quantities of food were being assembled for the feast within the longhouses:

So in we went through the small opening which takes a mighty stride to step over, for the door step is three feet high and there is no door, and then to be confronted with an acrid smoky gloom, with phantom forms moving hither and thither, and sunbeams sending their shafts through roof holes in silver pencils; and then as the eyes grew accustomed, the pupils expand on surely the strangest scene that they have ever looked upon. The phantom forms resolve themselves into hideous furies, hags and witches, moving hither and thither amongst great piles of bananas, smoked fish, sago and feast stuffs as though they were slaves of Moloch about to raise a sacrifice. These fearful crones are the women of the village, unbeautiful and ugly beyond belief. (Diary 2, 4 December 1922)

    Down the centre extended a long hallway, with small cubicles on either side which opened on to the main passage without doorway or partition, fishing nets, bows and arrows, dresses, and the characteristic belongings of all Papuans (Drums, pipes, etc.) hung from the roof and posts. The whole abode was orderly and clean. What amazed me greatly were the women. They wore strange caps with long teasled fibre pending down in tresses, which gave to them a particularly wild appearance, such as one generally depicts in Neptune's daughters and mermaids. These women however were very ugly, being smeared with mud on account of a recent death in the village. They also wore grass ramis, which appeared to add to the length of this grotesque head wear. (Diary 2, 2 December 1922)

    Down the long gloomy corridor McCulloch and I trod, those about us scarce heeding, for they were busy with the preparation of the feast and nothing else mattered. For 70 yards we walked pacing the great length and marvelling at what we saw. Such a scene have I beheld amongst the poor of Old Jerusalem; where poverty treads through darkened gloom and alleyways, with the primitive wares and foods hanging on either wall. In this great house families dwelt all on one common ground floor with neither privacy nor wall between them. Truly indeed it is a communal house, where all dwell together in peaceful and happy harmony. Amidst the bustle and gloom of this market-like corridor we moved, amidst the grass encumbered forms and men besmeared with mud, happy at the sight and peering into strange corners, examining native artifice and craft and seeing wonder in all that was commonplace. To record all this that no civilized being has previously seen would be the realization of a dream, yet it seems beyond lens and pen. The former I will try later, but the day and its scenes can only be a great memory.

    Much that we examined of the crafts of the natives show them to have attained to a fair stage of development. Their basketware is unexcelled throughout the Territory, and shows conspicuous originality in ornamental design. The fishing nets and hoop nets are admirable handicraft and as for the canoes, they hold first place on Papuan waterways. The people gave us much assistance and submitted to a process that to them, must have seemed meaningless mystery, and with no other rewards than half a stick of Ku Ku per exposure. (Diary 2, 4 December 1922)

V.4946

115

V.4950 *Women in mourning dress, Adulu village, near the mouth of the Fly River, Western Province. 2-5 December 1922.*

Hurley finally persuaded some women in mourning dress to pose for photographs on 4 December, but the poor light concerned him. On 5 December he discovered that the mortuary ceremony was already underway when he reached the village and some women had already disposed of their mourning dress.

Some time ago a notable man in the village died, and from henceforth the people have covered themselves with sackcloth and ashes, but the ashes in this case happen to be the ooze of the Fly and the sackcloth garments of teasled grass that wreathes the unfortunate females in hideous shrouds. This strange mourning garb is girdled about the body completely covering the breasts like a corset, clasps the waist, and then flows to foot, and trails behind. A cap is worn that suggests the furies in adding to the terrible aspect. Woven in a crown which caps the head and then falls down in long tresses behind where it mingles with the other teasling of the mourning garment. Grass widows-deluxe, excepting in looks, which are further beraddled with the slime of the Fly.
   We induced the women eventually, or rather a number of them to parade from one house to another — the death walk of the witches would be an eloquent title, but the sun was low and the sky cloud banked, so that I am dubious of the issue under the unfavorable conditions. Tomorrow I hope to try again. Tomorrow there will be rejoicing in the village. The feast will be set and the encumbrances of mourning will be cast aside and the female form in all its alluring subtlety will blossom again. Not so for me. If the feast could be but delayed a few days so that I might make the best of what few have seen, I would be muchly pleased. (Diary 2, 4 December 1922)

V.4952 *Two women in mourning dress, Adulu village, near the mouth of the Fly River, Western Province. 5 December 1922.*

I ascertained that the great collections of food which had been made in the communal house were for a feast, which took place during the day or early morning, and it "celebrated" the cutting off of the mourning raiment which was burnt immediately. However, we managed to discover a couple of the older hags still in their weeds and induced them to be photographed, which I did with fervour. I gave two sticks — a wealthy payment — of good trade tobacco to each one I photographed, and it was not long before all the females in the village turned out. Those I required I photographed and rewarded with one stick, they not wearing their weed. The women appear to be the masters of ADURU, which is not surprising, on account of their doing all the work. They make the fishing nets and do the fishing, dig the gardens and cook the viands, make the string and baskets and in fact do all the village work. Doubtless the men in times gone by merely kept themselves fit for fighting, making weapons and canoes. The village now has just passed that stage, and the men, not having any of these pursuits to occupy their time, are cheerful loafers. The donning and method of wearing the grass mourning interested me greatly. The cap is first put on, a small closely woven cap with a long teasled grass fringe which extends right to the heel and frequently trails behind in a short train. A long grass petticoat passes over one shoulder, diagonally across, and over one breast and pends to earth. A second grass petticoat is placed over the other shoulder, passes across the other breast, and likewise dangles to earth. The strings of these two garments where they pass over the shoulders gather in tightly the flowing grasses over the neck, producing a very witchy aspect. The lower ends of the petticoats are finally gathered up and drawn through the legs and fastened in the front in a clumsy bundle. The whole grass raiment suggests a grass widow very much run to grass; in fact were it not for the glimpse of the face, feet and hands, the women might be mistaken for moving grass sheaves. (Diary 2, 5 December 1922)

V.4939 & V.4938 *Longhouses on Sumogi Island, Fly River delta, Western Province. 5-7 December 1922.*

On its way back from Lake Murray, the expedition spent three nights at Sumogi Island at the mouth of the Fly River. In common with many peoples of the Western Province, the Sumogi people lived in longhouses on the banks of waterways. On arrival Hurley learned that eleven new canoes were to be launched the next day. The launching took place at dawn, without any obvious ceremony, while the expedition members were still asleep.

The village we found faced a small tidal and very pictorial creek; with tall coconuts growing along the banks and the canoes moored in the immediate front of the village. It is one of the most pictorial villages I have seen and quite justified our staying a few days. (Diary 3, 6 December 1922)

Of the canoes, two of which are shown here, Hurley wrote:

The canoes were of magnificent workmanship, their finish being equal to any I have seen in the Territory. Their lengths ranged from 40 to 50 feet, the latter capable of carrying 20 people. The prows were decorated with a carved board similar in design to the Koia carvings that we had observed at Kaimare. Being merely flat boards tapering like a very attenuated tombstone at the top, the bottom being cut square for lashing to the canoe prow. On the side facing the canoe a grotesque carving of the human face was well executed, whilst the back side was adorned with croton leaves and a strange tail of Cassowary feathers (this latter is also used for dancing decoration). Regrettably, the people were using steel axe heads set in the original stone adze handle, so much of the interest was lost. (Diary 3, 5 December 1922)
The canoes returned with the upflowing tide, and being informed that I was taking pictures by the whole village shouting all at once, came into the creek in fine style and pomp. Five canoes with decorated prows and painted, rowed by 18 crew each, with the whole village massed on the banks made a wonderful picture, and depicted the wild life as I have not filmed it before. The circumstance of launching the canoes and the return from the fishing expedition was fortunate, not only in the actual pictures that I secured of the incidents, but it served to dissipate any fears the villagers might have had concerning our intentions . . . . (Diary 3, 6 December 1922)

Having missed the launching of the new canoes, Hurley and McCulloch went ashore to the longhouse on Sumogi Island, where they found that most of the women had gone fishing. This provided "a good opportunity to go ahead flashlighting" inside the houses (Diary 3, 6 December 1922).

The village comprises one long communal house and two smaller houses, also a very small house on high sticks which I ascertained to be the home of the unmarried young men. The village reposed beneath the shade of fine coconuts and was less muddy than most places I have visited on the Fly. We went in to investigate the large "Long House" which we found in most respects similar to ADURU. The house of SAMAGI contained a much greater collection of nets, baskets and the characteristic chattels and belongings which I have described at Aduru. Bags hung heavily from the posts and rafters. Huge circular nets spanned the ceiling so that one had to bow to pass beneath them. The house was divided into two compartments, the large apartment being given over to the women, principally on account of them storing the whole family belongings, doing the cooking and general work, rather than the idea of setting the wife up in a mansion. The women's room contained also the foodstuffs and in fact everything appertaining to the actual living. It in turn was divided off into cubicles, each family having its allotted space, though neither partition nor division beyond a sapling separated the families. The people must dwell in much more neighbourly harmony than in our communities. Under such environment there is absolutely no privacy, but the free lives of these strange people I presume calls forth no necessity for it. They live and eat like animals, and have a moral code that none would dream of breaking. The men's quarters are separated by a division with a doorway in the centre. For some extraordinary reason these doorways are made so high that it is a great effort to step over, what is more like a window sill than a door step. The room was desolate of nets, bags and other impedimenta, being in fact absolutely barren. Excepting for bundles of arrows, bows, and a few axes. Like the women's apartment, the room was divided up, a single post serving for the partition. Thus it would appear that the women do all the village work, whilst the men purely attended to the fighting and canoe building. Now as there is no fighting the men stay at home and are more or less loafers, loafers on the women. (Diary 3, 6 December 1922)

The contents of this room do not match Hurley's description of the men's area, and may indicate that this was the women's quarters.

V.4939

V.4938

121

V.5207 *Allan McCulloch sending a wireless message on board the* Eureka. *5-11 November 1922.*

The exact date and location of this photograph are uncertain. If the wall calendar to the right of the clock is correct, the *Eureka* was somewhere between Daru Island and below Everill Junction on the Fly River, Western Province.

McCulloch, Ichthyologist at the Australian Museum, joined Hurley's party at short notice to collect biological and ethnographic materials for the Museum. A much-travelled and respected scientist, McCulloch proved an excellent choice, competent in his allotted task and in handling wireless contacts with the outside world. He was, furthermore, the only white person in the team with whom Hurley could establish a close friendship and rapport.

The wireless, supplied by Amalgamated Wireless of Australia, provided not only access to help in the event of an emergency, but also permitted Hurley to transmit reports for publication in The Sun newspaper in Sydney. To achieve this, messages had to be relayed from the *Eureka* via Daru or Port Moresby.

The photograph shows another important aspect of the expedition's technology; electricity. The use of a generator for electric light greatly eased work in the evenings, especially important to assist McCulloch in the processing of his specimens, and Hurley for writing his diary and press articles. The party soon learned, however, that the bright light had its disadvantages in attracting flying insects in great numbers. On several occasions, the insects became intolerable and the light was put out.

The 'armoury' included four .303 rifles on loan from the Papuan administration. On his first expedition Hurley had carried a rifle for protection, even noting in his diary on his first visit to Gabone at Marshall Lagoon that "I hopped ashore with my rifle", adding only later in pencil "and my camera" (Diary B, 6 April 1921). On the second expedition during which the party was visiting 'uncontrolled' areas without the benefit of armed police for protection, the party was at some considerable risk. This point was made to Hurley by Murray and other administration officials who loaned him additional weapons and advised the party not to go ashore unarmed (Diary 4, 15 January 1923). Ironically, this advice contributed to the seizure of Hurley's collections on his return to Port Moresby. While at Daru he showed a missionary photographs of the party carrying weapons on Lake Murray. The missionary, Riley, appears to have misunderstood the reason for the weapons, easily done since missionaries generally travelled unarmed, and reported the matter to the Resident Magistrate, E.R. Oldham. Either Oldham or Riley, or both, assumed that Hurley was obtaining ethnographic specimens by violence and armed threats, and reported the matter to the administration in Port Moresby. Hurley's diaries nowhere record such acts and explicitly state "we happily made no use of the arms" (Diary 4, 15 January 1923). The only times the weapons were used were to demonstrate their power to villagers — a common ploy even by government officers — or to shoot animals for museum specimens. The demonstration firing of a rifle on Lake Murray was particularly impressive (Hurley 1924: 400).

V.4909 *Entrance to the longhouse at Totani village, Aramia River, Western Province. 27-30 December 1922.*

The expedition entered the Aramia River from the Bamu River on Christmas Eve, 1922. On Boxing Day Hurley took on board a young man from an unnamed village to assist them in locating the Gogodala villages on the Aramia and its lagoons. They soon entered a lagoon in which the *Eureka* was halted by reeds. They attracted the attention of people in a nearby village, and were ferried across to the village of Uladu. There they spent the day and at 4 pm were taken across the lagoon to Totani village. They spent the night on board the *Eureka* and on 27 December set up camp near the Totani longhouse.

The Gogodala at that time were still occupying longhouses a hundred or more metres long which accommodated the entire population of a village. These longhouses were built on low rises on the banks of watercourses and lagoons, with small gardens alongside the house. Sago provided the main food, and was obtained from nearby swamps. Since Hurley's time the longhouses have been replaced by small houses for individual family units; A.L. Crawford (1981) has published a well-illustrated account of some of these changes and a reconstruction of the traditional life style. While Hurley noted several changes underway at the time of his visit (for example, see V.4912 and V.4915), his description of the longhouses at Uladu and Totani, and their setting, seems to reflect little change from contact with the outside world. His most detailed comments refer to Uladu:

On going ashore at the village new scenes of wonderment were to unfold. The village which comprised a single large communal house, was built on the crest of one of the rises which I have previously written about. It was enriched by a well laid out and kept garden, and by grass free paths. Everywhere was scrupulous cleanliness and order. It seems strange to fall in with a comparatively highly developed and aesthetically inclined people dwelling amidst such environment, the shores of a swamp in the heart of Papua. The gardens which encircled the house gave to it an air of great homeliness. In fact it was one of the few places which we civilised folk would regard as a home. The gardens were trenched and hillocked and planted in orderly rows, though the plants were a strange collection. Taro grew alongside crotons, Dracaenias Colei and potatoes. It was much the same as us growing vegetables and flowering plants in one bed. Arranged along the centre of the beds were uprights over which yams trailed, giving a very charming effect to the gay colored ornamental shrubs. This place is the first native village that I have seen where any attempt has been made to beautify environment by horticulture. The house which we were invited to enter, was a still more remarkable edifice; and though not as big as others we have entered was undoubtedly the best built place that we have seen. The timbers used were solid and unyielding and the framework, though entirely lashed with cane and vines was solid and perfectly rigid. The house was built up on piles about six feet high, though the roof from the ridge extended in an arched curve to the ground, making a large apartment below which I believe is used for storing and working in. The roof by this method also forms the side walls, it is thatched with sago palm leaf and perfectly water tight. The house is entered by the usual cross stick steps, and then a small verandah. The door is a mere pigeon hole nearly five feet up in the front wall. The "door step" is a piece of bamboo up on to which you step, wriggle through the hole and step on to a corresponding bamboo on the inside — then down on to the floor. By removing the bamboos and closing a flap door over the entrance, invaders would have a difficult time forcing the house. There is such a doorway at the opposite end. (Diary 3, 26 December 1922)

His detailed description of the house interior is given with negative V.4914. For Totani he provided only a summary description:

I have previously described the Communal House wherein these people dwell. My admiration for its construction has grown with closer examination. I append a section showing the arrangements of the various apartments. The women's cubicles occupy the entire length of the two sides. The men's loft also forms a ceiling to the main social hall. The whole constructional frame is lashed together with cane and is as rigid as if bolted. The entire edifice is remarkable for its rigidity and solid honest work in comparison with most other Papuan houses which are more or less lightly constructed and "Jerrybuilt". The views across the waters of Aramia Lake from the entrance to the communal house of Totani are beyond beautiful. The waters are broken by numerous islets and undulating rises all clothed in grass of verdant green. The rises are devoid of timber, doubtless due to their being continually burnt off and being used at odd periods for gardens. Here and there a coconut plantation of small proportions caps a rise or a brown thatched house rises from the long grass. It reminds one more of a charming English rural scene than a tropical landscape of swamp and savages. Just by the house is the gardens I have spoken of previously. The House caps the rise, and the gardens are made on the sloping sides, laid out in orderly rows and trenched, a precaution very necessary on account of the severe rains. Down the centre of each bed a line of high poles is placed vertically, so that the yams might trail their green vines over them. Taro is planted in rows with crotons and dracaena, the tout ensemble resembling a well kept flower garden gay with multicolored foliage. (Diary 3, 27-30 December 1922)

V.4914 *Interior of the longhouse at Uladu village, Aramia River, Western Province. 26-30 December 1922.*

Hurley's description of the Uladu longhouse continues:

The interior too was quite different to anything that we have hitherto seen. A great square space occupied the bulk of the house which was walled off on either side by sago palm stems lashed to uprights. This hall forms the general social meeting and living space, and is also used for ceremonial dances and purposes. There was on either side a row of cubicles formed by the outward curve of the roof and the inner wall. A narrow verandah way ran down either wall five feet above the main floor, and from it openings led into these cubicles — the dwelling places of the women and children. Before each entrance was placed a novel, compact yet efficient stairway made by deeply notching logs. Above this narrow verandah way further notched logs led up into the "attic", where a staging was placed on the rafters — this the sleeping place of the men. I am told that this is for defensive purposes, the men thrusting spears down into invaders passing beneath. "Fireplaces" were on the main floor, being just the conventional slab of mud on which small logs were placed. The smoke filled the house, but it drove out the mosquitoes and that was a small annoyance compared with the irritation of these plaguing pests. Everywhere superior workmanship was evident, there was no ramshackle construction, uprights plumb and joists level. The floor, which was made of slats of Goru palm overlaying close joists, was as solid as earth. This was the village of URADO. From its entrance a fine prospect looked out over the verdant rises and grass strewn lake waters to the far distant margin of the great jungle. (Diary 3, 26 December 1922)

This photograph, taken by flash, reveals some of the cultural changes taking place at the time of Hurley's visit. Only two, possibly three, men are wearing the conical cap *(diba)* indicating that a man has been initiated (see V.4912), though most of the males here would appear old enough to have been initiated. Several men are wearing mourning caps *(atima,* see V.4906). To the top right of the group hang two hurricane lamps, and one man has a metal knife thrust under his woven armband. Such goods may have been obtained by men working for Europeans outside the Gogodala area, or received as payment for services to government officials passing through the area. By 1922, although no government stations, missions or trade stores were operating in the Gogodala area, many men had been recruited for plantation work in the Central Province and on pearling luggers in Torres Strait. Government patrols into the area began in the early years of this century and by 1917 the area was regarded as almost under administrative control (Crawford 1981: 36-9).

V.4912 *Gogodala man of Uladu village, Aramia River, Western Province. 26-30 December 1922.*

Traditionally, each Gogodala youth would undergo a series of initiation ceremonies as he entered puberty. The fourth stage of the ceremonies allowed him knowledge of the *Aida* cults, and admission to the male secret society associated with the cult. In the first stage of initiation the boys were secluded in a special house away from the longhouse, observing food taboos and receiving instruction about their social group from their mothers' brothers. From these maternal uncles they received body decorations essential to the initiation and their life as initiated men: woven chest-, neck-, arm- and leg-bands, a conical cap, and various shell and seed ornaments (Crawford 1981: 246). The conical cap, *diba*, was attached to the head with wax or tree resin. Hurley observed these caps at Uladu village:

They rowed across in canoes after much deliberation and ferried us across to the village. The people were of medium stature, pleasant of countenance and hospitably inclined. Several wore strange conical shaped hats, which I am informed are placed on the head when married and are never removed. The hair grows into and is woven in with the meshing of the cap, surely indeed a most embarrassing encumbrance. (Diary 3, 26 December 1922)

At nearby Totani village he made further observations:

Not the least interesting item was the visit of numerous natives from more remote villages. They wore the characteristic conical caps which I believe were common to all, though now with the touch of civilization they are fast vanishing. This strange headwear, like a dunce's cap, is worn at all times, the hair is woven and grows into its texture and can only be removed by cutting off. (Diary 3, 27-30 December 1922)

To reduce infestations of lice, lime was poured in through a small hole at the top, and itching was relieved by putting a pointed bone through the hole and scratching the scalp (Crawford 1981: 49). In addition to his chest bands *(kawali)*, the man is wearing a mourning necklet *(madamamaka)*.

V.4912

V.4900 *Gogodala woman holding a fish basket, Totani village, Aramia River, Western Province. 27-30 December 1922.*

The world of the Gogodala is dominated by water — as lagoons, rivers and swamps. While providing prolific breeding grounds for mosquitoes, the waters also supply the Gogodala with food. Hurley did not make any observations on fishing techniques, but Crawford (1981: 91-3) provides an excellent summary of techniques.

   The Gogodala men take very little part in fishing. The lagoons are divided into clan and subclan areas, and a woman may fish only in the area of her husband's subclan though, with permission, she can fish in her father's area. Traps and nets are the main techniques; fishhooks are a post contact introduction. Several kinds of traps are used, the largest being that shown here (*sae:ya*). These large traps are used when the lagoon level is dropping and are set up in streams feeding the lagoon. Small weirs of sticks and grass help to direct the fish towards the trap. After setting up the trap, a woman will inspect it daily.

V.4900

131

V.4911 *Gogodala woman with fish trap, Totani village, Aramia River, Western Province. 27-30 December, 1922.*

In this photograph the woman shown in V.4900 has been persuaded to lift her mourning veil and reveal her face. Across her chest and shoulders are zigzag cicatrization scars *(kaka poleda)* probably made while she was very young and before she was initiated (Crawford 1981: 257).

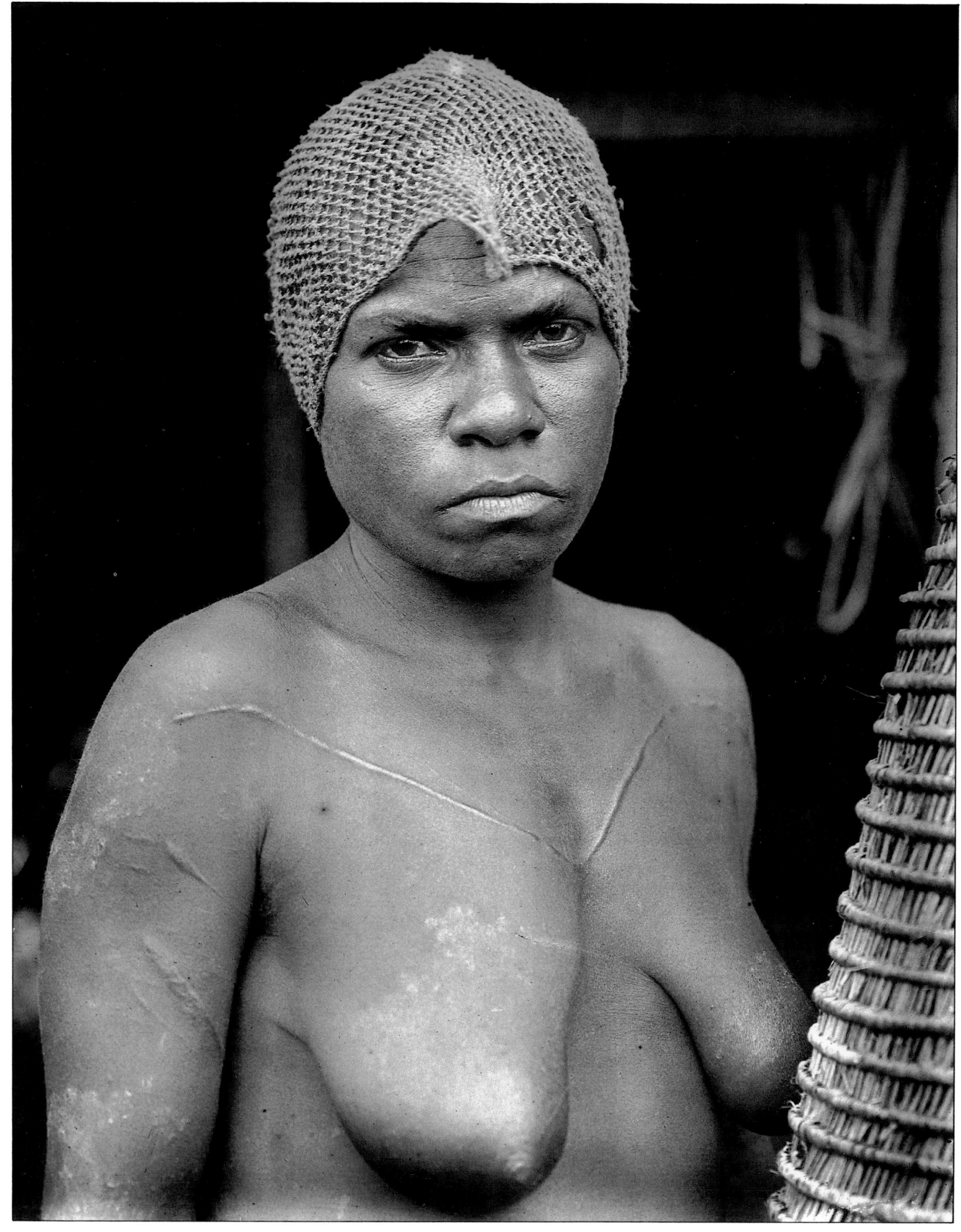

V.4911

V.4906 *Gogodala husband and wife in mourning, Totani village, Aramia River, Western Province. 27-30 December 1922.*

Hurley and McCulloch camped at Totani village for three nights, during which time the women were persuaded to pose for photographs. This couple is wearing a mourning cap and veil *(atima)*. The man is probably wearing a mourning skirt *(tao awalela)*.

The women after much persuasion were induced to pose. Those natives who had conspicuously assisted us brought their wives before the all seeing eyes of camera and cinema. The ladies were extremely shy and nervous, holding on to their husbands' hands and shivering violently. This is not surprising as the chief raiment was a coarse net worn completely over the head like a bag and a few wisps of grass elsewhere. (Diary 3, 27-30 December 1922)

Further down the Aramia, towards the Bamu River, Hurley saw a similar mourning headdress at an unidentified village:

I noticed a large number of women, through the glasses, peering at us from obscure shadows and observed many shrouded completely from head to breasts with the strange net-bag veiling which I have mentioned at Totani. In addition they wore long grass ramis extending from the waist to the toe. In this garb they looked extremely grotesque, even hideous. I am informed that this strange raiment is the garb of mourning. If this is so the entire village must be in mourning for all were so attired. Through close marriage everyone appears related, and as the garb is worn at least twelve months the hapless women are rarely without this wretched encumbrance. (Diary 3, 31 December 1922)

According to Crawford (1981: 50), the women would wear the long skirt until the second stage of mourning when a feast was held, possibly as long as one year after the death.

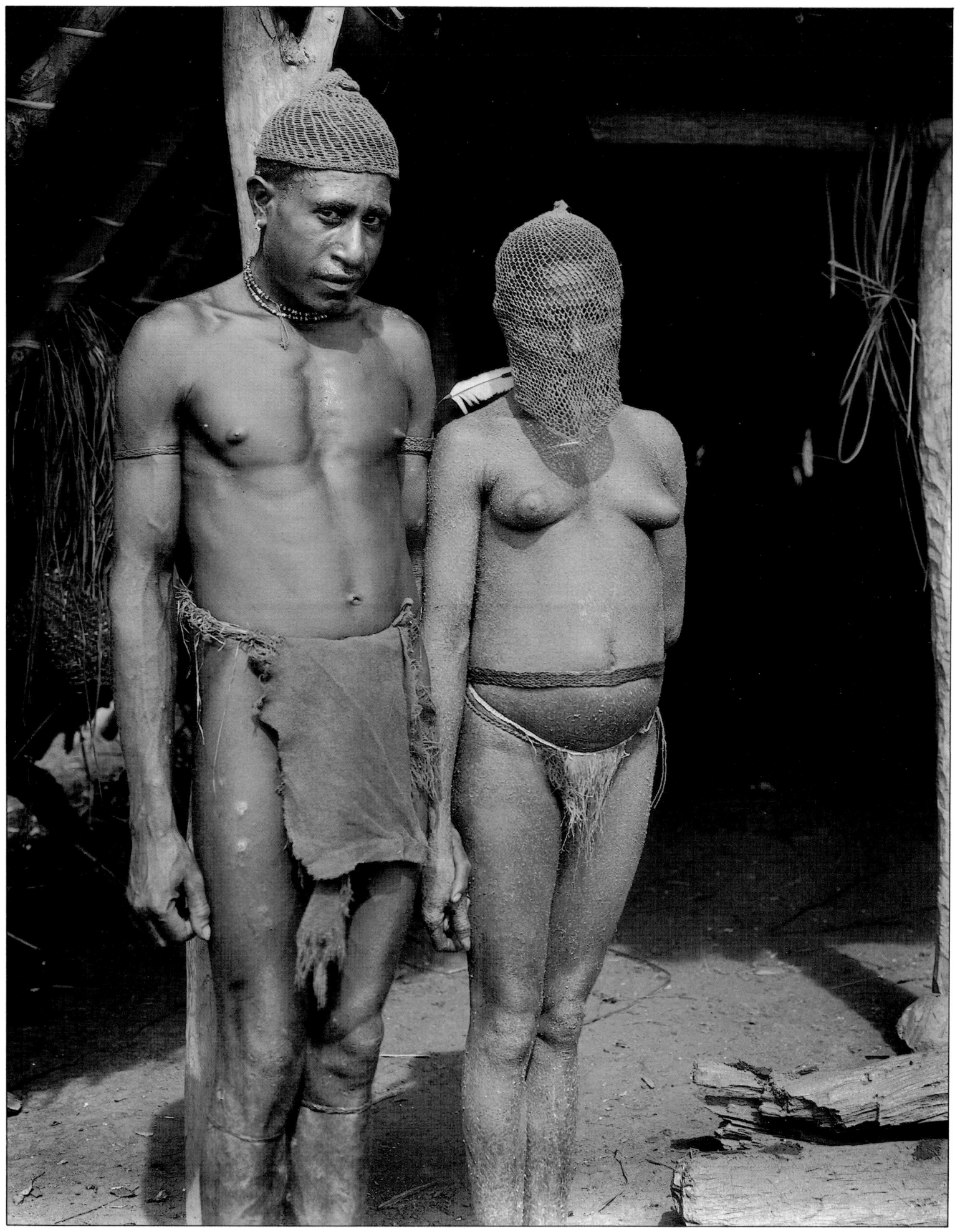

V.4915 *Gogodala canoe near Totani village, Aramia River, Western Province. 27-30 December 1922.*

Hurley lamented the fact that he saw little wood carving among the Gogodala, but was impressed by the canoes which were still elaborately decorated:

I had hoped to see more carving in the house (at Totani) but I am of opinion this art is being lost with the old men. Several canoes are ornated in the fashion I have shown two leaves back, but most now avoid this admirable practice and the crafts are purely utilitarian. I made several overtures to purchase one of these canoes for the Australian Museum, Sydney, but only small damaged ones were available or offered until on the eve of our departure our price was too much to resist and a new vessel finely carved was selected from the fleet. This canoe I had admired many times as being the finest on the Lake. Although it measured 40 feet I was determined to secure the prize and carry it on the deck of our already much encumbered vessel. The purchase price was: 3 calico ramis, 1 axe, 1 large knife, 1 small knife, 20 sticks tobacco. I further augmented this absurd request by empty tins, mirrors, beads, doubled the tobacco asked and sundry small presents. The canoe now reclines on the port side of our vessel where it most effectually blocks all passageway on that side and is universally cursed by the natives (in unheard and unexpressed thoughts). (Diary 3, 27-30 December 1922)

The canoe was off-loaded in Port Moresby (see V.4389), and eventually reached Sydney in September 1923. It is now registered as E.28332 in the Australian Museum. It measures 12.6 metres in length, and has the insignia of the *Kanaba* subclan (Crawford 1981: 340).

Although a cumbersome item for Hurley to collect, the length of this canoe is small when compared with the clan or racing canoes which can reach up to 30 metres in length.

Canoes were and still are the sole means of moving through the Gogodala area, though today they may be powered by outboard motors. The canoe shown here is a *taodanapa gawa* or man's canoe.

V.4389 *Unloading the Gogodala canoe from the Eureka at Port Moresby, National Capital District. 16 January 1923.*

When Hurley and McCulloch returned to Port Moresby on 13 January 1923 at the end of the expedition, they found the town full of "absurd and fanciful rumours of our adventures". They did not help the situation, for they told the crew of the government launch stories of their experiences "which we garnished profusely". On 15 January Hurley received a letter from the Acting Official Secretary, James Baldie, informing him that the Resident Magistrate in Daru, E.R. Oldham, "has reason for believing that some irregularities may have occurred in the securing of certain curios by your party at Lake Murray". Hurley had already received a wireless message while in the Fly River area that four crates of specimens consigned in the previous December to Sydney had been impounded; now all of the specimens on the *Eureka* were to be seized. Oldham was instructed to conduct an inquiry into the allegations, a process that could take considerable time and in Hurley's eyes, would be virtually useless in the absence of interpreters to communicate with the Lake Murray people. Hurley replied on 16 January, personally delivering the letter to Staniforth Smith, the Administrator during the Lieutenant-Governor's leave of absence, demanding that an immediate inquiry be held in Port Moresby with statements taken from the expedition members and crew. Staniforth Smith finally agreed, but the collections were still impounded on 16 January and were taken to the "local Museum" by a team of government prisoners. Hurley and McCulloch left Port Moresby on 26 January with the enquiry still incomplete. The matter was resolved only after Murray's return from leave, and following an acrimonious exchange of views between Murray and Hurley in *The Sun* newspaper in Sydney.

Not all of the artefacts were released to Hurley and the Australian Museum. According to *The Sun* of 21 March 1923, a number of bullroarers and a *kwoi* board were sent back to Kaimari village in the Purari delta. Since the Assistant Government Anthropologist, F.E. Williams, was working in that area, he may also have laid a complaint against Hurley. Williams had joined the expedition at Kaimari on 19 October 1922, to accompany Hurley to Lake Murray (Diary 1, 18 September 1922). However, when the expedition went to Daru to arrange the return of Lang, Hill and the 'Seagull' to Sydney (Diary 1, 25 October 1922), Williams, for an unexplained reason separated from the party. He subsequently published trenchant comments about the ways in which Hurley obtained photographs, and McCulloch artefacts, in Kaimari, though without actually naming either man (Williams 1923a: 1-2). The diaries do not mention any problems between Hurley and Williams; in fact, Hurley's comments about Williams are positive and complimentary, even though Hurley found Williams' concern to obtain accurate, detailed information at Kaimari irksome and, to Hurley's mind, not worthwhile (Diary 1, 19-20 October 1922).

Had Murray been in Port Moresby to handle the complaint against Hurley and McCulloch, he would probably have handled the matter more diplomatically and efficiently than Staniforth Smith and Baldie. Hurley seems to have had much respect for Murray and was well aware of the animosity displayed towards him by many other Europeans in Port Moresby (Diary C, 16-17 June 1921; Diary D, 15 August 1921).

Murray eventually released most of the artefacts, which reached Sydney in several shipments; the canoe arrived at the Australian Museum on 12 September 1923.

This dispute was not concerned with any failure on Hurley's part to obtain a collecting licence. Prior to leaving Sydney he had sought the assistance of the Director of the Australian Museum in obtaining a licence. The Prime Minister's Department referred Hurley to the Official Secretary in Port Moresby, and Hurley obtained it on 8 September 1922.

The matter did not rest with the release of most of the collection. In 1925 Hurley tried to return to Papua to make his feature film *The Jungle Woman*. Murray, however, set such restrictive conditions, including a ban on using local people, that Hurley abandoned the plan, eventually making the film in Irian Jaya, then under Dutch control. Furthermore, an unidentified reviewer of the book *Pearls and Savages* in *The Times Literary Supplement* of 2 October 1924, severely rebuked Hurley for the manner in which he obtained photographs of sacred figures at Kaimari. The reviewer pointed out that Hurley had taken an extreme liberty and if he had been caught, by traditional law he may have been killed.

V.4389

V.4930 *Longhouse on Morigio Island, at the mouth of the Turama River, Gulf Province. 2 January 1923.*

V.4227 *Skull display on the river bank at Kerewa village, Goaribari Island, Gulf Province. 3 January 1923.*

On the return from the Aramia River, Hurley first visited Bimaramio village on the Bamu River. Finding that most of the people were away making sago and those remaining were "uninteresting and unpictorial", he proceeded to the Turama River mouth and spent the night off Morigio Island. The *Eureka* had passed Morigio on 23 December 1922 when it entered the Turama River in error for the Bamu River. Hurley was anxious to visit the Gogodala people on the Aramia River and so did not stop. On this second visit to Morigio, the adverse tide prevented a landing and Hurley took this photograph from the deck of the *Eureka*:

The strong outrunning tide precluded us from going ashore, it racing by at three knots, but we were able to observe details of several remarkable "Long Houses". As I have already mentioned, these strange edifices shelter the entire village under one roof. The main road or hall passing down the centre and each family's stall or cubicle occupying an allotted space. The Long House at Morigio Island is one of the largest I have so far seen, it measuring by calculation from the vessel's deck, over 500 feet. A flotilla of canoes rowed out in their dugouts, and I was hopeful of securing stone adzes or weapons from them. The poor creatures seemed quite destitute and thinking we required the implements with which they excavated their canoes brought them out. I was chagrined to find the blades were of steel. Evidently all the stone adzes had been traded previously. They had little to entertain us, either in themselves or their wares so we wasted no time and set off for Goaribari, which is some 15 miles distant. (Diary 3, 2 January 1922)

The published version of this photograph has a flight of flying foxes superimposed on it. The flying fox negative was taken up the Fly River (Diary 2, 28 and 30 November 1922).

As the *Eureka* approached Goaribari Island, the engine broke down. Apart from the inconvenience, Hurley was disappointed that he was unable to proceed that night to Kerewa village where, he had learned, a ceremony was being performed. Temporary repairs to the engine permitted the *Eureka* to reach Kerewa early the next day, by which time the ceremony was finished and many of the visitors were already departing.

The hour was yet too early to use the cinema to advantage, but as soon as the opportunity presented itself I went ashore. The first objects that attracted our attention were small groups of skulls impaled on posts facing the river. These gruesome objects were tastefully decorated by a ruffle of palm leaves, rolled into scrolls at the ends, which maintained a shivering movement in the breeze. The skulls were provided with very long noses, more like long beaks, and the eye sockets were filled with clay and eyes made from small red seeds. The skulls were painted with raddle and were indeed grinning caricatures of death. We were extremely fortunate in observing this display, for such treasured belongings are hidden in the fastnesses of the Long House, and are only brought out on ceremonial occasions or to display to visitors the valour of the village. They appeared to me to present rather a warning to guests than hospitality. (Diary 3, 3 January 1923)

V.4930

V.4227

141

V.4236 *Interior of the longhouse at Kerewa village, Goaribari Island, Gulf Province. 4 January 1923*

Hurley visited the longhouse on 3 January, when he wrote his description of it; this photograph was probably taken on the following day when he "spent most of the day flashlighting the interior". The village consisted of the main longhouse and a series of smaller houses occupied by the women. Hurley was allowed to enter some of these and compared them with the scene inside the longhouse. The buildings were linked with each other and the shore by a raised wooden walkway apparently built as a result of government pressure to provide a less muddy means of moving about the village than by walking through the mud.

From the vessel an admirable view is presented of the great Long House which extends along the river bank for no less than 500 feet! This great structure is well and solidly constructed from lashed saplings and timbers thatched with the leaf of the sago palm. The edifice stands some 5 feet off the ground on quite a jungle of piles and is, excepting in height, the largest house that we have yet seen.

    This sapling track first passes the entrance to the Long House which we will enter and leave by its far doorway. The doorway is larger than usual, and one can pass through without having to climb up and over the style like door step. The vastness of the hall causes one to loiter on the threshhold in wonderment. Like a vast tunnel, the gloom extends to the far end where it is pierced by a star of light the farther doorway diminutive by perspective. Extending down the entire length is a great promenade some 18 feet wide, which is kept clear of all impedimenta for the free passage of the inmates. On either side cubicles are arranged, mere areas bounded by uprights and cross sticks without partition as we understand the word; nor is there privacy from neighbours or passers excepting for the gloom, which semiobscures all things. Above each cubicle and extending the full length is a narrow ceiling which serves for the stowage of goods and chattels. The tenants sleep on the floor, generally placing a palm leaf sleeping mat beneath them for a mattress, and a log of wood for a pillow. Each cubicle has its small slab of mud for a fire and many contain small shrines on which clusters of skulls are placed.

    I observed no work going on in this great building, which was entirely devoid of women and children. The men simply idled, smoked or slept and gossiped. Our passage incited little comment, and the inmates showed themselves willing to explain or show us the use of everything.

    The building was well floored with beaten out stems of the sago palm and altogether was clean and less smelling than I would have imagined. The view from the far end back to the entrance, with the light striking in feeble beams through small side doors on to reclining groups, and the black figures moving to and fro in the semi-darkness, made even a striking appeal to our faculties which now are become blase to all things except the most extravagant. We will now pass without this great "Hall of Indolence" by one of the small side doors, and climb up a notched pole on to the sapling pathway. It will be observed that the road of sticks follows parallel to the entire length of the Long House, and that on its other side is arranged numerous irregular groups of houses, similar in external construction to the Long House itself. These are the abodes of the women. As we pass by, a few coyly leave the small porticoed verandahs in front to peer through cracks and crevices, but most remain where they sit to smile and gossip amongst themselves as we pass. It appears from numerous enquiries that the wives of all the male members of a family dwell in the one house and that family life as we understand it does not exist. Seeking and gaining the permission of one of the men who chanced to be visiting his wife's house, we entered one of the houses to satisfy our curiosity. We found so much impedimenta dangling from the roof that it was necessary to proceed bowed double. The houses are rarely more than 30 to 40 feet long, and from the small doorway a narrow hallway leads the length to an exit at the opposite end. On either side small cubicles are arranged similar to the Long House, but in place of indolence here is activity. The fires burn smokily choking the acrid atmosphere, so that we could barely see nor breathe. The women were busy kneading sago, mixing with it mashed banana and rolling the mixture into sausages with outer coverings of leaf. These they laid on the embers and baked. I could not bring myself to sample the staple diet which smelt much like burned glue. On the walls hung fish traps and nets, whilst from the roof pended inverted cornucopia like receptacles, woven from fibre which I was informed were for the holding and parcelling up of sago. The women here are ever busy. They are bought like merchandise and become slaves to the indolent males. When the food was cooked, the women carried it to the Long House where the hungry lords awaited. (Diary 3, 3 January 1923)

V.4233   *Man of Kerewa regrinding a stone adze, Goaribari Island, Gulf Province. 4 January 1923.*

By the time of Hurley's visit, ground stone adzes had been replaced by metal ones, and the use of stone was essentially a thing of the past. He was fortunate, however, in photographing

. . . . one of the old original types grinding a stone adze and swinging the blade, I also gave the old man a chipped blade to face up: after spending some six hours on the grinding it showed very little improvement. (Diary 3, 4 January 1923)

   The adze blades shown here, with their quadrangular cross-section, probably were obtained by trade, through many intermediate links, from the highlands of Papua New Guinea. Hurley was able to purchase some stone blades at Kerewa:

When the light was good enough we again went ashore and continued photography and collecting. I was gratified beyond words at our success in being able to purchase stone adzes from the natives. When they learned that we were willing to pay ten sticks of tobacco a blade, these souvenirs of their grandfathers came forth in great numbers, so that we made an excellent choice of some magnificent specimens. These blades are shaped in perfect symmetry and are of highly polished basalt. The labour in a single blade must have taken months, yet steel supplanted it, and these worthless souvenirs of the young men will propitiate worthily the memory of their grandfathers in the Museum show case. Altogether we secured 16 blades, one, a perfect gem, I would not exchange for a blade of gold. (Diary 3, 4 January 1923)

V.4228 *Skull rack inside the longhouse at Dopima village, Goaribari Island, Gulf Province. 3 or 5 January 1923?*

This photograph is attributed to Dopima village but Hurley's diary entry states clearly that when the *Eureka* reached Dopima they did not go ashore because of the low tide level. It seems more likely that the photograph was taken at Kerewa or later at Babai village to the east. At Kerewa he recorded that:

These shrines have a backboard carved with a crude human face and on a small shelf in front the skulls are arranged. I expressed a great desire to purchase some of the skulls for the Museum collection, and though I offered a pound a head, tobacco, rice, calico, etc. etc. plus persuasions and threats, the owners were unwilling to part with them. They thus expressed themselves: "The Government now forbids us kill more victims and so we are deprived of the means of getting more and will not part from those which we have." These, however, were only the old and ancient warriors; the young men, changed by contact with civilization, would have sold the lot at a stick of tobacco a head. (Diary 3, 3 January 1923)

On leaving Goaribari Island for Urama Island, Hurley decided to stop at Babai village, to inspect a newly-constructed longhouse. The expedition spent part of the day there taking photographs, before proceeding on to Urama Island.

There was a particularly fine skull shrine near the entrance to this long house, and I tried every possible ruse to secure it precisely as it stood. I offered two pounds and 100 sticks of tobacco, or rice, armshells, knives, axes, or whatever the owner might desire. I was put off by being informed that the owner was away making sago. As I saw many interesting items here for the cinema I informed the people to send for the owner, and I would trade with him. The son of the owner arrived late in the afternoon, and I displayed the purchase price before him — 100 sticks of tobacco, 20 lbs rice, 5 ramis, 5 strings of beads, 5 white cowrie shells, 5 Bidi Bidi (head of cone shell), 1 axe, 1 large knife, 2 large arm shells, but all these enticements availed not. The son of the owner informed us that if he disposed of these things his father would be annoyed on his return and also that the old men would kill him by puri puri! To test the truth I placed a large and tempting bundle of armshells with the rest of my offerings: this was too much for the young fellow who without hesitation acquiesced. As I was desirous, however, of reserving these for more important use, I was regrettably unable to secure the shrine and its skulls. (Diary 3, 5 January 1923)

V.4223   *Woman of Goaribari Island, Gulf Province. 3 January 1923?*

Although described only as being from Goaribari Island, this woman was probably photographed at Kerewa village. Hurley "seized the opportunity to pick out the most characteristic types and for the payment of one stick of tobacco wanted not for willing sitters". This woman was so willing that Hurley photographed her at least three times, wearing different body ornaments and waist cloths. The glass plates of the other two views are held by the National Library of Australia, Canberra.

The woman was clearly posed for Hurley. It is not clear which ornaments she may have worn on a daily basis but, since Hurley visited Kerewa at the end of a ceremony, she may have been specially decorated for it. Other women were also decorated:

The women load their arms with the highly valued armlet shells (sections cut from cone shell) and adorn the breast with shapely crescents cut from the Mother of Pearl Shell. This treasured ornament which can only be afforded by the well to do, is suspended by a string round the neck, which is attached to either end of the crescent. Then the ladies wear many rowed necklaces of beads and band their shaven crowns in a manner that must be a sore encumbrance. (Diary 3, 3 January 1923)

V.4221 *Man of Goaribari Island, Gulf Province.*
3 January 1923?

As with V.4223, this man was probably photographed at Kerewa village.

The Goaribaris are conspicuous by the amount of ornate trappings which they wear, chiefly made from shells, and I must admit they are competent in the art of display. No Goaribari is dressed without his leggings which fit the calf tightly and are adorned up the front by two rows of small cowrie shells.
    The men are of medium build, well proportioned, and look as though food were abundant. The women are not as ugly as those of the Fly and a few might be regarded as comely — but a very few. Perhaps if they wore a little more clothing they might be more attractive, for apart from a grass belt and a very narrow V of fibre, even less than a fig leaf, they are unclothed. The men wear more, a large cumbersome V section cut from the bailer shell, a very ornate belt of carved bark, and a strange bundle of teasled fibre or grass, that falls behind like a bushy tail. (Diary 3, 3 January 1923)

V.4240 *Carving an arrowhead, Babai village, Gulf Province. 5 January 1923.*

Leaving Goaribari Island for Urama, Hurley visited the newly-constructed longhouse at Babai village, at the mouth of the Aird River. Inside the longhouse:

The inmates were all idling, excepting for a few old men making arrow heads. This process was extremely interesting, as the points were being shaped and barbed by the use of a mollusc shell. The adeptness in the use of this crude knife excelled the user of a steel blade, and it is notable that this implement which nature has cast up on the beaches in vast profusion should be still used, ay even preferred. (Diary 3, 5 January 1923)

Hurley persuaded one man to work on the beach, with a canoe as a seat, and posed him teaching a younger man.

V.4240

153

V.4753   *Village scene on Urama Island, Gulf Province.*

V.4762   *Start of a canoe race at Urama Island, Gulf Province. 9 January 1923.*

The mouths of the Kikori, Purari and several smaller rivers form an extensive delta at the head of the Gulf of Papua. Urama Island lies in the middle of this area. Hurley visited Urama twice: in 1921 with R.A. Woodward, Assistant Resident Magistrate based at Kikori Station, and in 1923 with Allan McCulloch on the *Eureka*. The first visit, of two nights only (25-27 June), was hampered by wet weather, but Hurley was able to take photographs in the large men's houses, *daima,* called *dubu* by Hurley.

Going ashore I was amazed at the frightful squalor and desolation of these Urama villages. Built but a few feet above the tides, and subjected to the incessant rainfall, they were little more than quagmires. The sombreness and gloom fairly got on one's nerves. Wherever one stopped it was squelch through mud and filth. Through years of accumulation debris and refuse had built up the ground around the houses, and were it not for this heaped garbage there would scarce be a square foot on which to walk. Our landing struck me as being quite unique. We stepped from the dinghy on to a canoe, and a score of natives came down and glided us by wading through the mud themselves and pulling the canoe up to the village garbage banks. The problem of improving these villages which the Resident Magistrate has to face is an unsolvable one. Decay on these mud flats is so rapid that if the place were corduroyed it would only last a year at the limit. The houses are being incessantly repaired and platforms leading across mud streams have to be renewed constantly. The life of these people is a constant strife with decay and a struggle for existence. Interminable rains add to their misery. The houses are as is to be expected built up on piles. (Diary C, 25 June 1921)

Hurley's comment on 'corduroy' refers to the government-induced practice at Kaimari and other places, of building raised walkways between houses and the various sections of a village. Urama lacked such walkways except for small bridges over creeks. Hurley's reception on the second visit was warm:

At lunch we eventually dropped anchor off the two villages Kinomere and Tovei. These two Urama villages are pictorially situated on the banks of a small tidal creek and present an enchanting picture. Two years ago I visited these villages and was impressed by the pristine condition of the people and the villages. Traders scarcely seem to have visited the place which is unaltered in any way from its original state, excepting that the people are peaceful and now friendly inclined.
 When it was explained that my object in visiting them was merely to study them, make pictures, and purchase curios, we became very popular. Many of the natives also recognised me through having visited them on a former occasion, and when it became known that I was in the flying machine that had passed over their village I became an object of universal curiosity. (Diary 3, 6 January 1923)

Throughout his travels, Hurley was fascinated by the various canoe styles and organised canoe races at several places. On his second visit to Urama Island he held a race for one-man crews:

I offered a prize of a large armshell for the winner of a single man canoe race and a stick of tobacco for all entries. The news spread instantly and at once the village was abustle. It hummed with excitement like a disturbed beehive. Canoes shot out from obscure recesses under the trees and everyone that owned a paddle from tiny toddlers to toothless dodderers entered. The single man canoe is one of the queerest barges — for it is little thicker than bark — that ever floated. The characteristic vessel measures up to 14 feet long and is barely more than a span wide. The equilibrium can be upset with the little finger much less by a heavy man standing upright. Seventy five canoes entered and took up their line above the village. So close were the canoes marshalled that there was barely sufficient paddle room. Alongside the *Eureka* a line was run out between goal posts and marked by a flag. At the signal of a revolver shot the canoes got away very badly owing to the extreme congestion. The river was alive with a mosquito fleet and it seemed impossible in the commotion that overturns could be avoided. From the beginning, a single figure shot ahead and maintained a two lengths lead until the winning line was reached. One of the local lads acted as judge, there was no refuting the decision, and the armshell was handed over amidst great acclamation. The stick per man was presented and everyone left for home happy and contented. (Diary 3, 9 January 1923)

All the formalities were observed in this race; note the Australian flag in the centre of the river and the starting line — a piece of rope stretched across the river.

Most of these canoes were single man craft, about 10 feet long and simply excavated trunks barely more than foot wide. The hull was rounded, entirely without keel or outrigger, and the freeboard no more than two or three inches! The rower stood erect and used a single broad bladed paddle to propel this extraordinary craft. The while, the paddle-man maintained his balance instinctively, much as a bird on the wing. The canoe almost seemed to become part of the man, so deftly was it handled and balanced. I purchased the best of the single man canoes about us for the Museum, paying 25 sticks of tobacco, 1 Mirror, 1 Rami and a string of beads. The owner took his craft ashore, and re-raddled and decorated it. We then lifted it aboard, a single man lifting without effort, and placed the novel addition inside the large Aramia canoe which encumbers the vessel. (Diary 3, 6 January 1923)

The canoe is now in the Australian Museum, registered as E.28333.

V.4753

V.4762

155

V.4777 *A group of dancers in front of the* daima *at Kinomere, Urama Island, Gulf Province. 7 January 1923.*

V.4776 *Four* keveke *dancers in front of the Kinomere* daima, *Urama Island, Gulf of Papua. 7 January 1923.*

Hurley had seen the large ceremonial masks of Urama on his previous visit and decided to film part of the ceremony on his second visit. This he arranged through 'Coir' (Kaea'a), one of the clan leaders of the Kinomere *daima*. The large masks, *keveke* (called *kaiva kuku* by Hurley), were used in initiation ceremonies for men, who would pass through various steps at certain times of their life. Women were not permitted to witness these ceremonies.

Almost break of day the obedient spouses left the village in canoes and went "bush". The dance which the men were going to perform must not be seen by woman or child. The village sounded abustle; everyone was putting on feathers, shell ornaments and decorating with raddle. I lost no time in going ashore and as soon as the sun was sufficiently high, the cameras and paraphernalia were loaded into our 'Canoe' dinghy, and with a flag fluttering astern, ourselves titivated with beads, we ostentatiously rowed away from the vessel. At the landing stage a crowd, wonderfully made up, formed a guard of honour and conducted us through the village to the Dubu. (Diary 3, 7 January 1923)

The men are seen here outside the *daima,* on an open space where they were to perform for Hurley's cameras. At this stage the *keveke* masks were still in the *daima*.

Hurley witnessed only part of the ceremony.

Providence was indeed kind, for my stage was made just in front of the Dubu, a low flat surrounded by higher ground, so that I might look down into the stage as from a dress circle. The high Ilima trees did not seriously obstruct the sunlight, and the background of the Dubu itself completed and perfected the arrangements. I took up a commanding stance and at a given signal the dancers filed out, dancing the while on to the stage which nature had set. I marked an area with saplings (the field of my camera), and with Vaieki interpreting and the indispensable Bormi acting as producer. A white assemblage of actors could not have done better. I was greatly pleased with the ready response to my desires and the attitude of the people to readily assist and carry out my wishes. The dancers seemed to intuitively comprehend what was wanted and worked to its accomplishment. The monotony of the dance was relieved by its brevity. The dance appeared to proceed in short sets — each appearing to differ from the other only in slight alteration of chant. The dance chief Coir and his understudy, an ancient veteran of 'the toe', performed the very realistic and wicked dance of the Witch Doctors. The expression and actions were perfect, but these two old men appear witches at any time. As the men had the village entirely to themselves I enquired if the Kaiva Kuku masks might promenade for the benefit of the white people. The head of the Dubu was an intelligent old chap, one named GORMIER, and it is due to the kindliness of this old man that I am indebted for the remarkable film of the Kaiva Kuku and for many other favors besides. Gormier discussed with the old men and finally after much deliberation they assented. This strange dance takes place but once in every seven years. It has rarely been seen by whites and never photographed. Further, the Kaiva Kuku masks are not allowed to leave the Dubu until after the dance, when they are all burnt: if any man should die during the interval between the dance ceremonies, his Kaiva Kuku must be buried with him. So that it will be seen that the people granted me no small favor in bringing forth these things, which must never see the light of day until after the ceremony. Strange then, that the women might look upon the masks, but no woman might gaze upon them until the ceremony has bereft them of the insidious spirit. The warriors arranged themselves in a circle and squatted down chanting and drumming. The Kaiva Kuku came from out the Dubu and danced in short jumpy steps into the centre of the ring of swaying bodies and heads. Then began the same caperings only turning round, facing one another, drawing close and then separating. Were it not for the extraordinary masks and their fantastic decoration the whole ceremony would have been dull and uninteresting. The purport of the ceremony I know nothing of, nor could I find out. But I surmise it is of the same nature as the initiation of new members into the Masonic Order. (Diary 3, 7 January 1923)

When he tried to purchase two *keveke* masks he was fortunate to obtain some old ones which had been used in a ceremony but not destroyed afterwards.

I paid another visit to the Dubu during the afternoon and endeavoured to purchase two Kaiva Kuku masks. Old Gormier informed me that this was contrary to the regulations of the Dubu, for the Kaiva Kuku might not be disposed of until after the ceremonial dance. If a man died during the interval the Kaiva Kuku must be interred with him. The old chap intimated that there were several masks in the houses that had been used at the previous ceremony and that they would be repaired and repainted for me. This was accordingly done, and when evening fell the Kaiva Kuku were brought out and paid for 20 sticks each (tobacco). (Diary 3, 9 January 1923)

These are probably the two Urama masks identified as *semese* in the Australian Museum, registered numbers E.27690 and E.27691.

V.4777

V.4776

157

V.4784 *Interior of a* daima, *Urama Island, Gulf Province. June 1921 or January 1923.*

The date of this photograph is uncertain. If taken in 1923, it probably shows the interior of a Kinomere *daima,* of which there were two at that time (R. Vanderwal, pers. comm). In 1921 Hurley had photographed the interior of at least two *daima* but complained that their occupants would not keep still and might ruin the photographic images.

Hurley does not appear to have taken any photographs of the *keveke* masks dancing inside the *daima* in 1923, but recorded it in writing:

A great commotion of dancers and chanting was going on inside. The chant was led by the M.C. or dance chief, who piped in a highly pitched falsetto then the whole assembly of dancers took up the theme in chorus. It sounded just like a teacher and a kindergarten, and it was difficult to realise that the voices were those of grown men. Let us see what is going on inside. Up the notched stick that serves as a stepway, on to the platform and then back beneath the small door and in to the gloom. Ye Gods, what a stupendous and amazing sight. A couple hundred dancers arranged in long lines down the length of the hallway, the light from the doorway glinting on decorations and glistening eyes, the diffused half light faintly throwing up the setting of great Kaiva Kuku masks and grotesque carved gopi, and the eyeless sockets from the skull racks, the only beholders besides McCulloch, myself and interpreters. Nothing I had seen during my previous visit equalled this spectacular, grotesque and wild gathering. The dancers ceased as we entered, and my rapturous enthusiasm and praise fired them to no small extent. We had expected perhaps 20 or 30 dancers; here were a couple of hundred! Anxious to display their ostentation, the leader pitched forth a few discordant tenor notes in to the gloom, the drums tommed, the massed voices chorussed, and each figure moved in rhythm with the whole. As a dance it was poor, but collectively the effect was remarkable. The white feathers, hinged to sway with each movement of the head danced, the headdresses of cassowary danced, the elbow plumes danced, everything responded in unison to the time of the drum beats, even the house jigged so that each movement gave us alarm lest the floor might collapse. The eerie gloom of the Dubu and its dark recesses glorified the impression, which amongst all the strange scenes in the gallery of memory hangs above the "line". (Diary 3, 7 January 1923)

V.4784

V.4785. *Skull rack with* gope *boards and crocodile skulls inside Kinomere* daima, *Urama Island, Gulf Province. 8 January 1923?*

The date of this photograph is uncertain. On 8 January Hurley noted in his diary that he had photographed a skull rack which he wished to purchase for the Australian Museum.

The first impression is of fantastic masks and carved shields dangling in semi-darkness and a large party of wild people squatting on the floor, reclining or smoking. A few sticks of trade tobacco put one on good terms and then for sight seeing. Extending the length of the Dubu is a long hall, twelve feet wide and as high as the roof. A large vestibule space is left at the entrance for meetings and social purposes then the hall begins. On either side of the entrance to the hall is placed a skull rack. A series of pigeon holes for the reception of skulls. These are the trophies of battle or chance victims. Each rack contained some 30 human skulls. Beneath the racks, carved shields are placed called GORPI, and on the floor by the Gorpi rows of pigs skulls and crocodiles skulls, souvenirs of the hunt and prowess. The Gorpi represent the spirits of ancestors and the object in placing them beneath the racks is to enslave the spirits of the victims to these ancestral spirits. Passing along the Hall, a vast collection of the huge Kaiva-kuku ceremonial dresses and effigies pends from the roofs, half obscuring the small cubicles on either side. These cubicles are extremely gloomy pens partitioned off with slabs of bark, yet wholly open to the main hall. Each had its small rack of skulls. . . . . . Also bows, arrows, drums, and the belongings of the tenant. Once the men resided here entirely, but the practice is given up to a large extent, they now going home instead of staying at the Club overnight. I was greatly impressed by the excellence of the carvings on many of the Gorpi, and the freedom and diversity of design. Many of these were crude, but others were worthy of better publicity and use than the dark unseen and unappreciated recesses of the Dubu pens. I intend remaining here several days in order to do some justice in recording these remarkable people and also collecting their artifice for the Museum. (Diary 3, 6 January 1923)

I decided to spend the day flashlighting the interior of the Dubu and opening negotiations for what I was reticent about mentioning previously to the people, skulls. I modified my flashlamp to operate with the certainty that it lacked, and after showing it working to the natives, they understood that no harm was intended them and they submitted — nay assisted. I arranged groupings in the Dubu, had racks altered and settings made to realise my wishes.

When the flashlighting was over I made council in the remote end of the Dubu and started preliminary negotiations for the purchase of a complete skull rack of 24 skulls, the GORPI shields pending beneath it and the pig skulls which were arranged in a long row at the bottom.

The price I said they could fix themselves. I intimated that I realised fully what these trophies meant to them. Each one was a record of a deed of valour, each GORPI a tablet to a dead brother, each pig skull a treasured souvenir. If it was against the law of the Ravi then I must go without; for I did not wish to impose nor digress from what might be their religion. GORMIER was obviously relieved by my last remarks and also understood quickly that we were not going to make playthings of their most treasured of all possessions. He asked questions about the Museum and was satisfied that we were genuine. I said I should like to take the whole partition from the Dubu — skull rack and all. The old fellow left us and went down to talk with the other veterans who were seated smoking in the vestibule. A short while after he returned, and said that the laws of the Dubu did not allow of any part of its structure being removed. If the partition were cut out a new Dubu would have to be built. He had spoken with his brothers about the heads and other things and they had agreed all to do as he would do and desire. He could not give me his rack of 24 skulls. These were the inheritance of his children and must be passed on; but he would help me. The old man rose and took from the rack one of his best skulls; he pondered affectionately over the terrible object, then untied one of the Gopi from its setting and selected one of the largest pig skulls, these he placed in a small pile and placed them beside me. GORMIER then called the names of the warriors individually, they entered their small cubicles and did as he had desired. It might seem strange that I felt rather sad about the whole affair; to secure a head from a head hunter might sound a permissible action to most people; but when it is understood that many of these skulls were relics passed down by ancestors — fine old warriors — heads won in fair combat — by strength of arms and valour and objects of religions reverence, it is natural that many must have felt a deep pang when parting with them. One young man spent fully ten minutes allowing his eye to roam over the 36 skulls which his brave father had won.

Henceforth each rack will have a vacant hole, perhaps it will remind them of the strangers who passed their way, but I am sure it will ever be a space of regret. The little bundles were all brought and laid down on the floor of GORMIER'S cubicle. On each I placed twenty-five sticks of tobacco, four bidi bidi and one armshell. I asked Gormier if the purchase money was satisfactory. He assented. Then the same question was asked of each they all assented, and the transaction — surely one of the strangest of trading incidents — was closed. Nor did the interest of the people wane here. They tore fibre from the Dubu decorations and helped to pack the skulls and tied up the GORPI. I expressed a wish to have a rack made exactly similar as to that of GORMIER'S. The old men went away and late in the evening the rack was brought out, complete in infinite detail even to the crude little decorations of queer figures and totemic symbols. This is the first occasion that I have experienced, where such punctuality and contract keeping has been adhered to by natives. The Urama people have topped the palm in my estimation and have my esteem and admiration. McCulloch is in his seventh heaven; for having secured such a prize has justified his accompanying me in the eyes of the Museum Trustees. I have added an improviso to my wishes concerning the exhibition of collection, and that is that the Museum Authorities will display the collection in the Main Hall and not bury it in the gloom of the cellar storeroom. (Diary 3, 8 January 1923)

V.4786 *Two basketry figures in front of a* daima *at Tovei, Urama Island, Gulf Province. 26 June 1921.*

Urama had separate *daima* for married and unmarried men, according to Hurley, but these may have been different clan groups. Hurley states (Diary C, 26 June 1921) that he only saw basketry figures such as these in the unmarried men's *daima*. Newton suggests that they may have been *kanipu* figures, comparable to basketry figures on the Era River east of Urama, and that they were used to enforce bans on taking coconuts needed for ceremonial feasts (Newton 1961: 19,78).

The unmarried men dwell in an immense hall called a Dubu — the Urama Dubu (unmarried men's Dubu) is some 30 feet high and 200 feet long. Going inside through a small square opening, which is overhung with a screen of stranded fibre, one enters a long passage way. This passage is walled on either side with the stem of the sago palm. Small entrances lead from the main passage into cubicles wherein the men sleep. An after passage leads into an open porch which is hung with an immense variety of remarkable masks, drums, bows and arrows, and all kinds of dancing rig. (Diary C, 25 June 1921)

In the unmarried men's Dubu of Tovei, I noticed several immense masks made from split lawyer vine which are used to terrify the women and children. I have not yet been able to secure the reason for these strange objects. These wickerwork masks were twelve feet in length with an additional two feet of frayed-out fibre from the Pandanus palm around the bottom. The person goes inside, his arms protruding through armlet holes in the wicker. As he dances about the "Goa" nut seeds secured to the neck make a harsh rattling sound. The dancer certainly looks very terrifying and uncanny. I also noticed another mask which fits over the head onto the shoulders, in the form of a cassowary. The right arm of the operator is thrust through the hollow neck and so controls the movements which are gone through with wonderous precision. (Diary C, 26 June 1921)

Referring to the mask roughly illustrated on the 26th June I learn that the mask is one of the methods of acquainting the people of a village — Kinomere and Tuv-ei in this case, that a ban or Taboo, is to be placed on coconuts. The men inside the mask rush about the village scaring the women and children, who run off screaming to the shelter of their huts. The mask is believed by them to contain a spirit who will make them violently ill if they should eat of the forbidden fruits. As there are but a few coconuts struggling around the villages, and the younger generation are very prone to pull the fruit before maturity, this means of placing upon the trees the taboo is efficacious and even when the fruit fall of their own accord they are not even eaten — no matter how hungry they might be until the Taboo is lifted. The figures, so attired, are highly grotesque and their fearsome appearance is an apparition that evidently makes a deep impression of evil forebodings should those transgress from its orderings. (Diary C, 1 July 1921)

V.4795 *Man of Urama Island wearing mourning bands, Gulf Province.*

The date of this photograph is not known. The Australian Museum Photography Register identifies the chest bands as a sign of mourning, but none of Hurley's descriptions of dress and ornaments mention this.

On the head is worn the characteristic Urama headdress. This wild token is made of two plumes of Cassowary feathers joined on to a narrow band. The band passes across the forehead, is tied behind the head and the two plumes rise slightly above the head and trend back in a stream line effect. The hair is matted into innumerable curls like a mop with grime, each curl terminating in a mud or wax blob. The hair is also generally decorated with two white Cockatoo tail feathers, secured over the crown and trending forward. The stems of the feathers is split, so as to delicately hinge and sway to and fro in the breeze or when the wearer moves about. Two large ear-rings of boars tusks, or woven from the central stem of cassowary feathers, and a large "nose bone" pushed through the septum, made from clam shell completes the head dressing — No, there is the painting. There appears to be no law governing this decorative art; it might extend to painting black circular spots around the eyes, or to daubing the entire face with red ochre, or a modification as the wearer inclines. Strings of beads in festooning necklaces girdle the neck, and a large half or quarter moon crescent hung from the horned tips rests on the breast. Bandoliers of plaited fibre adorned with a central line of small shells, cross from shoulders to under the arms. They are generally united front and back like a double pair of braces. The arms are girdled with arm shells and the private parts are hidden beneath a large V section cut from the bailer shell. This is fastened over the hips by a girdle also made of fine shells.

Around the waist the exquisitely carved belt, with a dirk stuck in askew, made from the thigh bone of the Cassowary. Exquisite leggings fit elegantly the calves, woven from fibre and adorned down the front with two rows of small cowrie shells placed back to front. A long bundle of teasled fibre is secured under the waist belt and extends over the "rump" like a bushy mare's tail. (Diary 3, 6 January 1923)

V.4867 *Aerial view of Kaimari village, Purari River delta, Gulf Province. October 1922.*

Kaimari was one of the main villages of the Namau people who occupy the islands of the Purari River delta. Hurley visited Kaimari twice on each expedition. In June 1921 he spent one night there while going to Kikori, but did not land, and later returned for two nights with Mr R.A. Woodward, Assistant Resident Magistrate at Kikori. On the second expedition Hurley's party stayed for two weeks with the *Eureka* and the 'Seagull' sea-plane, during which time they were joined briefly by Mr F.E. Williams, Assistant Government Anthropologist. The final visit on 10 January 1923 was for one night on the journey back to Port Moresby.

For the third visit Hurley arrived at Kaimari in the 'Seagull' with Lang as pilot on 6 October 1922. There they met McCulloch who had brought the *Eureka*, arriving only an hour before the 'Seagull'. The party stayed at Kaimari for two weeks, during which Hurley went up in the 'Seagull' three times, once to fly over Kikori to drop a message for Williams to join the expedition as soon as possible. The date of this photograph is not known, but Hurley's annotation states that it was taken at about 450 metres. Of the first landing at Kaimari on 6 October 1922, Hurley wrote:

Passing low over a maze of winding waterways Lang made a graceful sweep over KAIMARE — one of the most unique — perhaps the most — habitats of humans. The great Ravis stood out boldly and as the tide was high and the mudflats covered, the village appeared as if it had recently been inundated by a flood. The structures seemed to rise out of the water, and the various 'suburbs' or isolated parts were connected together by bridgeways. A desolate and gloomy place — yet fascinating. We swept lower and lower, receiving many bumps until we came over the fine waterway in front of the village. Lang made a beautiful landing right alongside the *Eureka*, frightening several canoe loads that paddled frantically out of the way. (Diary 1, 6 October 1922)

During his second visit in 1921, Hurley sketched the layout of the village in its three sections (Diary C, 28 June 1921). Each section had its own *ravi* or men's house, and a number of ordinary houses. Since Hurley's time the eroding action of the Purari has modified the islands shown here, and Kaimari no longer exists. Its inhabitants have relocated to another site (Vanderwal 1983).

V.4867

V.4824 & V.4873   *The 'Seagull', Gulf Province.*
12 October 1922.

Hurley first had the idea of using a plane during his visit to Kikori in 1921. Of the two planes taken to Papua in 1923, only the 'Seagull' was used outside Port Moresby, and then only at Kaimari. Lang took the plane up several times for sightseeing and aerial photographs.

Lang and Hill spent most of the time trying to maintain the 'Seagull' in the extremely adverse tropical conditions. The wooden floats and the fabric covering of the wings both suffered badly, and eventually the plane was sent back to Australia.

The 'Seagull' was the first plane seen in the Gulf of Papua. At Kaimari the local people presented a pig to the plane as a sacrifice to honour and/or appease it (Hurley 1924: 256, 259, 310).

During the afternoon the ceremony of sacrificing a pig to the flying machine was performed. The pig was shot by the owner with bow and arrow in the side. The pig at once made off pursued by a large crowd of hunters all armed with bows and arrows. They chased 'Dennis' across mud flats under houses and bridges, and finally brought him to earth after firing many arrows. The pig was then carried triumphantly along the 'Styx' Road, much as a funeral procession, only the head men taking part. Finally the pig was taken aboard canoe and rowed out to the machine. Lang and Hill were both aboard to receive the offering. A bag was placed on the bow and the pig laid thereon. The machine look uncouth with this strange offering on the altar like bow. The sacrifice was allowed to remain until dark when it was removed by us and presented to our native crew. This was the highest honor that could have been shown the Seagull. A pig is regarded as being more valuable than human life. The Government has stopped the sacrifice of human life and the pig is now substituted. The natives fully believed the machine would devour the pig overnight, but if they could have seen the crew whacking into it, I doubt if we would have been as popular. We ourselves did not sample the offering owing to the filthy feeding of the Kaimari pigs. (Diary 1, 11 October 1922)

Although the 'Seagull' did not visit Urama, its flight over the area to Kikori to deliver a message to F.E. Williams made its presence known widely. When Hurley later revisited Urama on the *Eureka,* he was greeted as a special person because he had been in the plane (see V.4753). It is possible that the 'Seagull' may have contributed to new occurrences of the so-called 'Vailala Madness' of the Elema area east of Kaimari (Souter 1963: 151). The leader of the cult, Evara, in 1919 had a book with a picture of a plane on its cover, and the plane seems to have become a symbol of the cult. Williams, however, took the view that the 'Seagull' made no impact on the cult (Williams 1923b: 10).

V.4824

V.4873

169

V.4854 Kau ravi, *Kaimari village, Gulf Province.*

The date of this photograph is not known. The walkways over creeks and mudflats were the result of government pressure and were also seen on Goaribari Island. Hurley described Kaimari as follows:

. . . . went ashore into the KAIMARE villages which line the seafront in rows two deep. Kaimare like Urama is a village of the mudflats though having been under government control for a much greater period it has been greatly improved. The rainfall also is not near so persistent and the means of moving from house to house can be done in comparative comfort owing to a raised roadway of corduroy. A forest of stumps has been sunk into the mud and on the framework mangrove saplings have been laid to form a continuous pathway. After the night's rain, however, I found the sapling roadway very slippery with moss and as the saplings are simply laid on top of other sapling supports, they have a habit of rolling under one's feet: occasionally a sapling through age and decay gives way under ones weight and it takes all ones balancing abilities to avoid being precipitated into the mud. The houses are very similar to the Urama people, only perhaps larger and instead of a straight ridge pole it is curved very much. (Diary C, 28 June 1921)

Apart from the obvious benefit of helping to keep one clean, the raised walkways had a more important role of reducing the risk of exposure to hookworm, and other parasites and diseases, since the mudflats served as latrines for both humans and village animals. Williams (1924: 1) described the mud as being "thanks to the more concentrated activities of men and pigs, a composition best described as muck". Yet this apparently unsavoury substance had a role in Kaimari subsistence:

Kaimare alternately appears as if flooded then with the low tides, as if squatting amid a desolation of mud. Pigs and infants squelch through the mud, thoroughly enjoying the hunting of crabs and small fish. (Diary 1, 17 October 1922)

On his final visit to Kaimari, three months later, Hurley found the walkways had deteriorated badly for want of maintenance (Diary 3, 10 January 1923).

V.4818 *Men of Kaimari village trading with the* Eureka, *Purari River delta, Gulf Province. 10 January 1923?*

V.4820 *Man using a stone-bladed adze, Kaimari village, Gulf Province.*

On his last visit to Kaimari, Hurley noted in his diary that on their arrival, many canoes came to meet them, their occupants wishing to trade bananas, pineapples, taro and sweet potatoes. His party also obtained many artefacts:

I secured a vast collection of arrows, beautifully carved — the work of bygone days — paying half a stick of tobacco each and also secured fine stone adzes at 10 sticks each. (Diary 3, 10 January 1923)

On this short visit the villagers seem to have been particularly anxious to obtain Hurley's trade tobacco, which he used liberally in payments for goods and services. On the second expedition he took about 200 kilograms of tobacco, issued from government stock, for use as a trade item (Diary 1, 24 September 1922). The list of stores for the expedition does not include any tobacco, cigars or cigarettes for the expedition party, perhaps because none of them smoked on a regular basis. By the end of the expedition, however, McCulloch had taken to smoking a bamboo pipe *(baubau)*:

. . . McCulloch puffing on his Bau Bau — a horrible custom of inhaling which he has adopted from the natives . . . . (Diary 4, 23 January 1923)

The *baubau* is a bamboo tube, with a small hole near the closed end into which a roll of tobacco is placed. One person lights the tobacco and then draws on it to fill the tube with smoke. The smoke-filled tube is then passed to another person who inhales the smoke.

The date of V.4820 is not known. The scene was almost certainly posed, for by the time of Hurley's visits to Kaimari stone tools had been replaced by metal ones, and the canoe looks as though it has already been finished.

These craft are remarkable for their instability and efficiency the latter being entirely due to the skill of the crew. The canoe of the Delta is merely a hollowed out log some 16 to 18 feet long. The dugout is open along the top and being round-bottomed turns over with great facility. The back of the canoe is open, and to make it water-tight a small mud barrier is patted in. Scarcely better is the front of this bizarre vessel. The canoe falls so low in the front that if it is propelled at sufficient speed the water is scooped inboard. To prevent this a small boy squats there, his back to the direction in which the canoe travels, and the caulking between the canoe and the boy is made with mud. This latter is of a peculiarly tenacious nature, it is the first and most plenteous material available. (Diary 1, 9 October 1922)

Hurley witnessed two canoe races at Kaimari, the first in 1921 and the second in 1922:

During the afternoon we had a canoe race, five canoes turning out, their occupants all decorated up for the occasion. Most of the canoes were rowed by 18 men. The rowers all stand up, each alternate man using his paddle on either the starboard or port side. The action of 18 men striking the water with their paddles in shovel-like motion drives the canoe ahead with a series of impulses, each impulse raising the canoe up and down. The prow is built up with a small mud bank, and immediately in front is seated a small boy with back to the water, who acts as a sheerwater and breaks the bow wave from coming aboard. The five canoes entered into the spirit of the race, enthusiastically, and the foremost could easily keep pace with the launch which was covering 6½ knots. (Diary C, 28 June 1921)

The second "regatta", in 1922, consisted of 25 canoes each with a crew of ten men. The course was a figure of eight round the *Eureka* and "Seagull". (Diary 1, 9 October 1922)

V.4818

V.4820

173

V.4857   *Entrance of Kau ravi, Kaimari village, Gulf Province.*

Although this photograph is undated, it may have been taken in 1921. There were three *ravi* houses for initiated males in 1921-2. In 1921 Hurley visited an unfinished *ravi* and noted that the entrance was open and that inside:

. . . . to commemorate the finishing of the roof the interior was highly decorated with numberless KOI-E (Gorpi). (Diary C, 29 June 1921)

In 1922 he revisited this *ravi* and found that the entrance was now closed by coconut fronds and that the men inside were making masks (Diary 1, 7 October 1922).

The *ravi* of Kaimari were 180 to 200 metres long, and about 20 metres at the entrance, decreasing in height to about 3 metres at the rear.

The constructional details of these great Ravis is highly complex and display skill and vast labour. Two lines of posts support two false ridges which extend the whole length of the structure. Heavy saplings are strained from the main central ridge to the flooring joists. These curved ribs are placed every three feet apart the whole length of the Ravi. Battens are lashed transversely to the ribs and extend from front to rear. The whole framework is covered with Nipa palm leaves from the stems of the palm and using the stem as a backbone the leaves are simply bent over and pinned on, using strands of split lawyer vine for the purpose. These sections are lashed on to the battens, and placed one beneath the other similar to the laying on of tiles. The floor is a network of mangrove saplings notched and bound together and covered with GORU palm the stem being beaten out flat. The whole of this ponderous structure stands on a forest of piles sunk in the mud. It takes the whole occupants (50 to 60) of the Ravi six months to construct their abode and as decay is so rapid, at their slow rate of labour, it must take the other six months to keep the ravi in order. Nipa palm roofs in this climate last two years at the most. They are perfectly water-tight in spite of the deluging rains and if they had longer life and did not harbour so much vermin, they would be difficult to beat for this climate. (Diary C, 28 June 1921)

Hurley published another view of this *ravi* entrance with a coconut leaf barrier blocking the view inside, presumably taken on 11 January 1923, when Hurley witnessed part of an *aiaimunu* dance (Hurley 1924: 287).

V.4835 *Interior of Kau ravi at Kaimari village, Gulf Province.*

In view of Hurley's comments about the Kau *ravi* in 1921 and 1922 (see V.4857), this photograph probably shows the interior of that *ravi* in 1921.

V.4841   Kwoi *ancestral boards with a crocodile skull, Kaimari village, Gulf Province.*

This photograph was probably taken inside Kau *ravi*, possibly in 1921 when the interior of the *ravi* was decorated only with boards and crocodile skulls (see V.4835).

The *ravi* was internally divided into a series of cubicles on each side of a central passageway, with a communal open area just inside the entrance. The cubicles *(larava)* were named and each was associated with one of the cane figures referred to in V.4838. The *larava* were the sleeping areas for men of the *ravi* belonging to specific descent groups and contained skulls of pigs and crocodiles caught by hunting, as well as the carved and painted wooden *kwoi* boards representing the ancestors of the *larava*.

The *kwoi* boards apparently were not sacred like the *kaiemunu* cane figures and were openly displayed; one appears on the verandah of a family house in V.4875. Sacred objects such as the *kaiemunu* and 'bull-roarers' were concealed in a closed cubicle at the back of the *ravi*. Hurley had difficulty in obtaining information about the *kwoi* boards, and even Williams (1924) who spent more time eliciting information obtained only an incomplete picture.

At the foot of each upright supporting the roof ridge were collected several KOI-E. These were hung near the ground vertically as shields, immediately below them were placed collections of the skulls of alligators and pigs, also food offering — coconuts and sago and the bailers belonging to canoes. It is a hopeless task endeavouring to unravel the whyfore of the customs of these people. I have tried numerous people to try and wheedle the purport of the KOI-E "shields" from them but each tells me a different story. It is so characteristic. Piecing all together I place most reliance on the following story which might serve to indicate their meaning: A man belonging to this same village set out in his canoe for upriver, where he intended to do some pig hunting. Some distance from the shore the canoe began wobbling and making a devious course, which rather amazed and startled its occupant, who knowing that his father had died recently and also that he had not placed a KOI-E in the DUBU to the honour of his memory, turned back and set about making one. Duly the KOI-E was completed and hung with the numerous other entablatures in the Ravi. After which being done the man went about his pig and alligator hunts successfully and without further molestation from the spirits of the dead. The skulls of animals captured in the chase were placed at the bottom of these KOI-E evidently to propitiate them for the believed successes of their forays. The KOI-E are not made today and I don't think the young men understand their significance. Many of the men from Kaimare have been at service with whites and have imbibed something of their ways and they are inclined to make little of their fathers' beliefs. The Dubu with all its dancing masks and KOI-E arrayed so that their painted sides face the entrance, is reminiscent of a museum adorned with ancient Egyptian coffin lids. (Diary C, 29 June 1921)

The board on the right is similar to canoe prow boards such as those mentioned by Hurley on canoes at Adulu, Fly River delta (see V.4939). Williams (1924: figures 15, 16) shows a range of *kwoi* forms but does not discuss canoe prow boards.

V.4838 Kaiemunu *cane figures inside Kau* ravi, *Kaimari village, Gulf Province.*

In 1921 Hurley was shown at the rear of the *ravi*:

. . . . a small partitioned off room wherein was contained a number of extraordinary masks resembling alligators. These are used in conjunction with a ceremony known as "KAIVA-KUKU" - which is connected with the initiating of the young men into the manhood of the tribe. (Diary C, 29 June 1921)

In 1921 Hurley was accompanied by the Assistant Resident Magistrate from Kikori, and a number of police. But in 1922 he found access to this secret section of the *ravi* more difficult:

At the far end of the Ravi was a partitioned off section which none might enter, this was in charge of a very hideous old chief. He considered for some time the advisability of letting us pass this barrier, then apparently reluctantly he bid us enter. In the darkness we made out that the place was filled with strange masks, something after the shape of a fish (known as Chaetodon). The masks were about four feet six inches long and 3 feet wide at widest part. The framework was made of cane and covered by a finely woven matting. The entrance for the body is at the bottom end. The significance of these masks is quite unknown to me, and I intend finding out as much as possible at a later date. On emerging from this Holy of Holies the old Chief demanded Kuku Kuku (tobacco). He informed our interpreter that unless a present was made to these spirits we would most certainly become violently ill and would die!! Not being anxious just at present we gave the old chief the tobacco as requested. Women on no account are allowed near the Ravi, which to me is quite understandable. (Diary I, 7 October 1922)

However, Hurley was determined to photograph these figures (*kaiemunu*):

McCulloch and I spent the day ashore in the village and in the Ravi. I was particularly anxious to secure pictures of the forbidden Holy of Holies at the far end of the Ravi. I took with me my coxswain Veiaki to interpret. There were very few in the Dubu so we walked to the far end presumably inspecting masks and details. This section of the Dubu or Ravi is held aloof from all young men and none must enter it. Whilst none were about Veiaki showed his contempt for their beliefs by removing the barrier and screen so that "the terrible spirits" stood revealed. There were eighteen strange effigies made of cane, evidently intended to resemble crocodiles. These were crammed together so that one had to crawl beneath them to pass through. This section of the Ravi was inexpressibly gloomy. The wind made a moaning sound through the leaf walls, whilst we disturbed hoards of bats, rats and lizards. I found it extremely difficult to photograph owing to the confined space. I exposed a plate by flashlight and we managed to re-erect the barrier without the inmates seeing us. Undoubtedly this would have ended in much noise and trouble had we been observed. I intend remaining here until there is sufficient sunlight to enable photographic work to be done. I have endeavoured to get up a dance, but as it is against local fashions and traditions I am afraid it is impossible. (Diary 1, 8 October 1922)

Hurley returned several days later when all of the men were absent from the *ravi* and took further photographs:

I spent the remainder of the day in photographing in the great Ravi, and secured many unique subjects, never likely again to be recorded. I managed to secure flashlights in the forbidden Holy of Holies, that remote screened-off end, at the distant part of the Ravi, in a strange and perhaps unfair manner. A person was dying in a nearby house, and all the populace were either there venting their grief or else out at their gardens. Veiaki, the indispensable, and McCulloch accompanied me, and finding the Ravi empty we at once moved to the Holy of Holies. The screen of coconut leaves we took down, and re-erected some 20 feet behind us, so as to give me ample working space and to hide our movements from any casual that might enter the Ravi. The Ravi at this end dwarfs down to ten and six feet. We discovered no less than seventeen huge masks made to represent alligators. These were all made of cane beautifully woven over stout frame work. They had four legs clawed at the bottom like a bird. An opening allowed a man to put his body through and so walk about with the mask covering him. Under each mask was a small packet carefully bound up in leaf. On opening it was found to contain a number of pieces of thin wood from 18 inches long to 9 long. These were obviously "Bull Roarers" which when whirled around the head make a roaring sound, the note according to the size of the "Bull Roarer". The sound produced is to represent the voices of the spirits of these mask effigies and terrifies the women and children. The old men endeavour to retain supremacy over everything which enables them to place a "Tabu" on the most choice of eatables, and in fact have a rare good old time at the expense of the uninitiated. This now is fast falling into disuse with the slow progress of civilization, and the enlightening which it brings. But tradition dies hard, and today the great majority hold steadfastly to their old customs, fears and beliefs. I am extremely fortunate in securing these pictures, for in a few years all these things will have passed away. No one appearing we moved one of the great crocodile effigies out into a more open position, so that a side view might be obtained. I secured a fine flashlight showing this individual mask, and also the general arrangement of the masks in the Holy of Holies. The natives began to return just as we finished and came up to see what we were about. Accordingly I handed McCulloch a packet of Tom-thumb crackers which he ignited and rushed out amongst the "intruders". The crowd rushed helter skelter in wild disorder pursued by McCulloch with the harmless crackers. The issue was a complete success for by the time the natives had recovered the barrier was back, and the Holy of Holies restored. The natives took the affair as a huge joke and laughed heartily over the incident — so did we. (Diary 1, 17 October 1922)

Hurley subsequently published one of these photographs in *Pearls and Savages* (1924: 307).

V.4838

V.4834 *Interior of Kau ravi, Kaimari village, Gulf Province. 10-11 January 1923.*

Hurley was particularly taken with the large constructed masks of Kaimari *(aiaimunu)* which he loosely called *Kaiva Kuku*. Convinced that such striking forms must be made for an impressive ceremony, he sought to have a dance held for him to film and photograph. His first effort in 1922 was unsuccessful:

During the afternoon McCulloch, Veiaki and myself visited another Ravi which was lavishly decorated with "Kaiva Kuku" masks. I gave several sticks of tobacco to the old men on entering, which had a welcoming effect. There was a large number collected in the Ravi whom I included in the pictures. I tried hard to arrange a dance, but it would appear that the dance will not take place for another twelve months, and anything which is not in keeping with the time old traditions and customs would bring terrible consequences down upon those who participated in it. Happily many of the young men have "signed on" for various periods, and many have returned from work with a broader knowledge. These manifested something of contempt for the pseudo beliefs of the elders and were for a dance, but the old men held out irresolutely. Nevertheless I am in hopes that the dance will eventuate, especially as I have offered big presents. (Diary 1, 9 October 1922)

The masks are unfinished: all lack the sago palm leaf skirt and several are only cane frames. In such a state they could not be used in a ceremony. But on his final visit to Kaimari, Hurley found the men of Kau *ravi* willing to stage a dance for him:

I have been desirous of having a large Kaiva Kuku dance made, and for this purpose went down to Kow Ravi to talk the matter over with the old men. A couple of hundred men attended this council and I interpreted to them that we had tobacco in plenty and would pay them well. Most flung traditions aside and were willing, but it nearly ended in a riotous disturbance before the elders were prevailed upon. A description of the construction of these Kaiva Kuku masks is interesting if only to indicate how trivially a population can indulge itself when it has no objective nor incentive to concentrate upon. The Kaiva Kuku ceremony is obscure. Questions from every source have failed — might just the same solicit information from a mason. Personally I believe it has much to do with the initiation of young men into the masonry of the tribe, and initiating them into the mysteries of manhood. Unlike our communities a young boy is ignorant and is kept so until this initiation takes place. Even then his knowledge but grows with his age and status in the tribe. The ceremony now only takes place at distant intervals, five years having elapsed since the last, and two more years until the next. The Ravi is encumbered with the great ceremonial masks which are constructed with infinite labour and care. The masks measure from five to twelve feet in height, and two feet wide. The framework is beautifully made from cane, intrically strutted, webbed and woven for great strength and rigidity with a minimum weight. Over this frame Tapa cloth bark is tightly stretched and stitched on. Then the design, of which the variety is endless, is outlined in fine split cane and sown on. This beautiful work is entirely freehand, there being no outlining or marking, the carvings are perfect and the complexity and freedom of design is marvellous. The cane outlining forms the pattern which is afterwards painted red or black, the background being made white. The designs are amazingly bilaterally symmetrical, which inclines one to the conclusion that the people are to a great extent ambidextral. As in my crude sketch two eyeholes are made, the nose taking up the form of a strange beak with rows of bristling teeth. The mask shape is conventional but the design runs the riot of the maker's imagination. There is no slovenly work in the making. Every section will bear closest scrutiny and one involuntarily feels what a waste of excellent labour! The work proceeds in stages and I am informed a feast is held before each of these stages can be entered upon. The back is covered with long stranded fibre, which overlay hoops; so that when the dancer is inside he is entirely hidden but for his feet. The entire congregation agreed to have the masks made ready, the Ravi platform repaired for dancing, and a platform erected for photographic purposes by tomorrow afternoon. The people will be compelled to hasten for once, for there is much to do and half a case of tobacco is worth striving for. (Diary 3, 10 January 1923)

V.4832 *Aiaimunu dancers at Kaimari village, Gulf Province. 11 January 1923.*

The front screen that closes the mouth of the Ravi from female gaze had been re-erectd to my desires, and most of the masks were made ready. This, judging by the drumming all through the night must have taken all the night to do. At 2 p.m. I took the cameras across, but there was much hesitation about putting the masks on. They expressed in wild hubbub that they would all die if the Kaiva Kuku were worn before a feast was made! Eventually this was overcome, but there was a demur about removing the front screen so that I might photograph.

The light was fast failing and the humbugging exasperated me. I cursed the lot to my full lung power, and threatened that we would at once go to Kikori and have the ringleaders put in gaol. This greatly disturbed the elders who amidst tumultuous clamour removed the screen. The drums beat, and a monotonous chant brought the Kaiva Kuku dancers from the gloom, into the light in front of the ravi. The dance was little more than a farce. The masks swayed from side to side in rhythm to the drumbeating and that was all! the combined effect was strangely grotesque but wholly disappointing. I had expected after all the labour involved in making the masks, to see something at least spectacular, but it was as much as I could do to turn the handle on the scene. (Diary 3, 11 January 1923)

Hurley's exasperation reflected his fundamental lack of understanding of the cultural change situation which confronted him. The situation was one of extreme flux. Hurley's lack of sensitivity to this situation may have contributed to F.E. Williams' strong response to Hurley's efforts to photograph the sacred masks of Kaimari (see V.4838), and to McCulloch's persistence in obtaining artefacts. Williams witnessed McCulloch's purchase of bull-roarers from Api *ravi* in October 1922. Both Hurley and McCulloch wrote accounts of the transactions. Hurley's account is as follows:

I mentioned on the 8th and 17th October entry of our visit to the Ravi near by, Ra, and of our experiences in the so-called Holy of Holies. I spoke of this gloomy containing 17 strange alligator like effigies, which the natives called IMUNU. Below these IMUNU were bag packages carefully tied up (one under each). McCulloch ascertained by untying one of the packages that each contained 20 to 24 Bull Roarers. He was also very anxious to secure a bundle for the Museum Collection. Numerous parleys failed to secure one of the bundles. The natives refused to sell or give, but it was suggested that one might disappear in the dark and a present left in its place. This was actually tried, but failed through other interested parties hearing of it. (Diary 1, 20 October 1922)

McCulloch's description is contained in a list of artefacts consigned by him to the Australian Museum (Australian Museum Archives M62/6: McCulloch to Anderson, 25 October 1922). Lot 42 consisted of:

No.42. Bundle of eighteen Bullroarers from the sanctum of the Ravi at Kaimari. 21.10.22. (two specially good ones are packed separately and are specially marked). This is a very special collection, and was only secured after much talk and threatening on the part of our interpreter. There were seventeen similar bundles on the floor of the screened-off portion of the Ravi at the far end, one below each of the large cane Imunu figures (see Hurleys photographs) each bundle belonging to a group of men who similarly owned the Imunu they were associated with. No amount of persuasion would induce the owners to part with any one bundle, they believing they would die if they parted with them. Much talk and some threats, however, persuaded them to allow me to open up each bundle and take out one from each under the supervision of an elder of the Ravi (I managed to get away with an extra one which accounts for the eighteen). Some bundles contained only twelve Bullroarers, most had more, and one had twenty three. Some were quite new, others old, and they varied greatly in size and shape. I was not allowed to select the biggest specimens, but managed to secure a couple of curiously carved ones which are packed separately. Most were without carving. The old man with me would not touch any of the bundles nor their contents, and I had to untie each one and rewrap and tie it after selecting a sample. When I brought this collection forward into the public portion of the Ravi nobody would touch it, and I learnt through the interpreter that I was expected to carry it on board the ship myself, each man being 'too fright he die'. At the front of the Ravi, they gave me a piece of palm leaf matting to wrap it in to hide it from sight, and they were well pleased when I further wrapped it in my shirt. On going outside I found the village almost deserted, only a few men along the pathway of sticks over the mudflats remaining to keep the women and children inside the houses. The keeper and some other elders followed well behind to receive the offering of seventeen sticks of tobacco and about three pounds of rice which I paid to the seventeen Imumu I had robbed.

Collecting these specimens was unpleasant work, being in a very obscure light, and numberless spiders, scorpions, and beetles, ran out of the bundles as I thrust my hand into them. I had to lie prone under the Imunu most of the time, there being rarely room to sit up, and all the time there was the knowledge that I was violating the genuine beliefs of a large crowd who would certainly have refused permission to even see these things had it not been for the fear which white men are held in villages which are "under control" by the Government.

These artefacts were among the specimens seized by the Papuan administration and taken to Port Moresby (see V.4389, V.5207). Some of the bull-roarers were subsequently returned to Kaimari, together with a *kwoi* board. Hurley, while regretting those returns, observed with some relief that at least the *kwoi* had been photographed and that "this is the next best record to the object itself" (*The Sun*, 21 March 1923).

V.4875   *A group on the verandah of a house at Kaimari village, Gulf Province.*

The house in this undated photograph appears, from the lack of thatching on the right hand side of the verandah, to be unfinished. In contrast with the men's *ravi* houses (e.g. V.4857), the ordinary dwelling house had a front wall in which there was an entrance. The houses were constructed facing the raised walkway through the village, with their backs towards the water. The verandah, formed by setting back the front wall, was the area where social activities at family level took place.

The woman seated on the right has daubed herself with mud as a sign of mourning. Behind the man is a *kwoi* ancestral board which would usually have been kept in the men's *ravi*. Above it on the house front wall is a carved circular decorative plaque similar to those visible on the *ravi* front of V.4857. The significance of these objects is not known.

The kind of house shown here was used by the wife and children of the family. Traditionally, the husband and initiated male children would have spent most of their time at the men's *ravi*.

V.4806 *Man in mourning, Kaimari village, Gulf Province.*

This undated photograph shows a man wearing woven string bands on his arms and across his chest and knotted string tassels from his ears which are indicative of mourning (Williams 1924: 47-8).

During Hurley's visit in October 1922, he saw a corpse laid out prior to the funeral:

The body rested on a sleeping mat made of pandanus palm leaf with the head to the east in the small sleeping apartment which I entered. The poor fellow was sadly emaciated and had evidently been sick a considerable time. The wives, three in number, were thickly coated with river mud from head to toe. (Diary 1, 15 October 1922)

V.4807 *Woman of Kaimari village, Gulf Province.*

The date of this photograph is uncertain but it may have been taken in 1921, when Hurley described the Kaimari women as follows:

Comeliness is as scant as their attire which is in the form of an insignificant bunch of grass, fore and aft, that one must look closely for to be aware of its presence. The nose is pierced and many were wearing a 'shell pencil' through the septum. Over the breast they wear a shell ornament made from the mother of pearl shell, three shells being used, the upper portion being cut away so as to form a crescent. The shells are laid one over the other like scales making a really beautiful ornament. (Diary C, 28 June 1921)

Since the 'mother-of-pearl' shell would not occur in the muddy waters around Kaimari, these shell ornaments (*mairi*) were probably obtained by trade, perhaps with Motu men from Hanuabada who visited the Kaimari area on their annual *hiri* trading voyages (Williams 1924: 125-7). The *mairi,* which could consist of up to six shell plates, was only worn on ceremonial occasions.

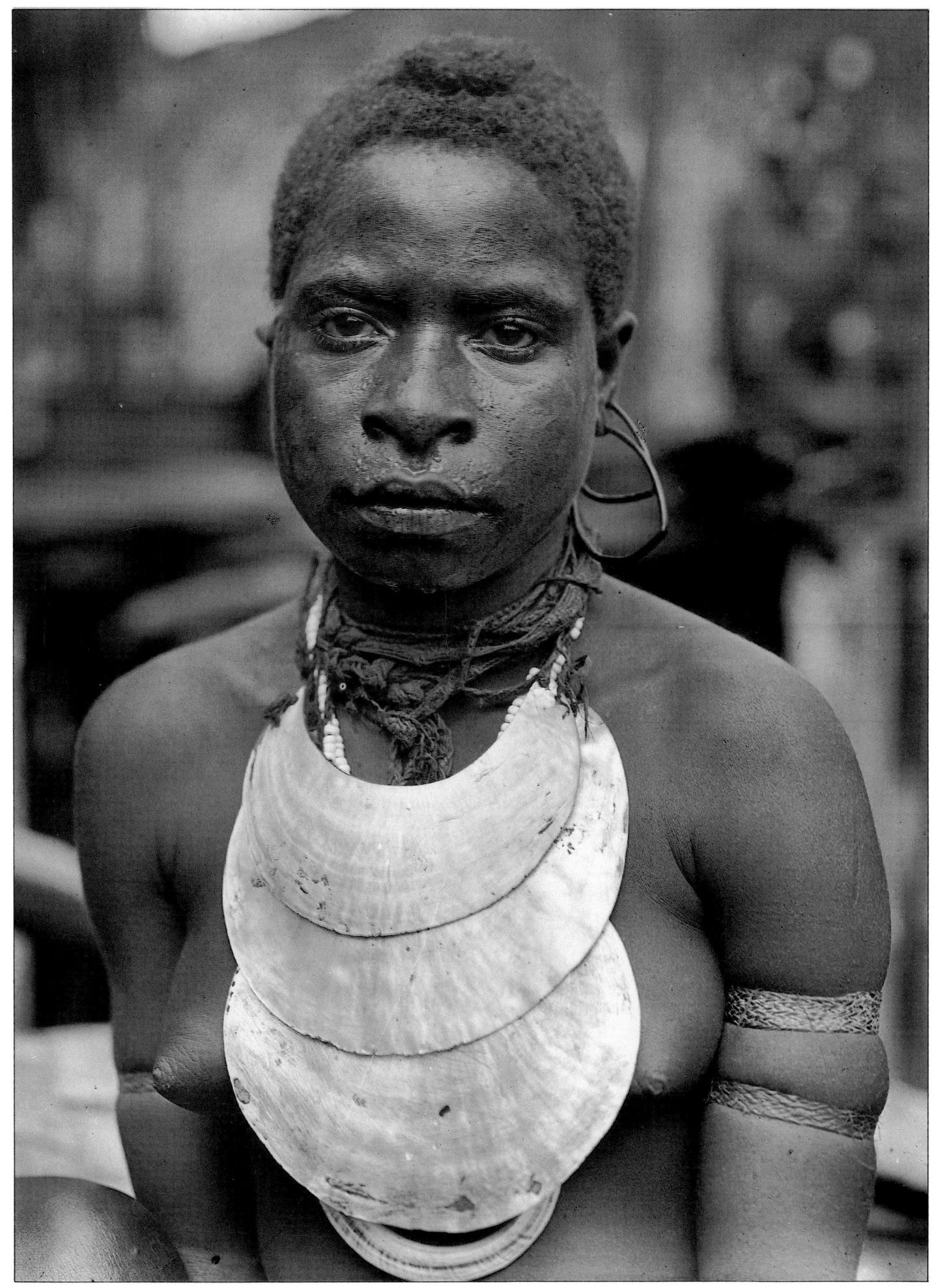

Bibliography

ALLEN, J. 1977. Sea traffic, trade and expanding horizons. In J. Allen, J. Golson and R. Jones (eds.), *Sunda and Sahul: Prehistoric Studies in Southeast Asia, Melanesia and Australia,* pp.387-417. London, New York and San Francisco, Academic Press.

AUSTRALIA 1914. *Papua. Annual Report for the Year 1913-14.* Melbourne, Commonwealth of Australia.

AUSTRALIA 1922. *Papua. Annual Report for the year 1920-21.* Melbourne, Commonwealth of Australia.

BICKEL, L. 1980. *In Search of Frank Hurley.* Melbourne, Macmillan and Co.

BARTON, F.R. 1910. The annual trading expedition to the Papuan gulf. In C.G. Seligmann, *The Melanesians of British New Guinea,* pp. 96-120. Cambridge, University Press.

BELSHAW, C.S. 1957. *The Great Village: the economic and social welfare of Hanuabada, an urban community in Papua.* London, Routledge and Kegan Paul.

CRAWFORD, A.L. 1981. *Aida: Life and Ceremony of the Gogodala.* Bathurst, Robert Brown and Associates in association with the National Cultural Council of Papua New Guinea.

DUPEYRAT, A. 1954. *Mitsinari: Twenty-one Years Among the Papuans.* London, Staples Press.

DUTTON, T. (ed). 1982. *The Hiri in History: Further aspects of long distance Motu trade in Central Papua.* Pacific Research Monograph No.8. Canberra, Australian National University.

GROVES, M. 1954. Dancing in Poreporena. *Journal of the Royal Anthropological Institute* 84: 75-90.

GROVES, M. 1963. Western Motu Descent Groups. *Ethnology* 2(1): 15-30.

HAU'OFA, E. 1971. Mekeo Chieftainship. *Journal of the Polynesian Society* 80 (20): 152-69.

HUMPHRIES, W.R. 1923. *Patrolling in Papua.* London, Fisher Unwin.

HURLEY, F. 1920-1923. Eight unpublished field diaries held by the National Library of Australia, Canberra. Manuscript nos. MS 883, items 7 to 13 and 33.

HURLEY, F. 1924. *Pearls and Savages.* New York and London, G.P. Putnam's Sons.

IRWIN, G.J. 1978. The Development of Mailu as a Specialized Trading and Manufacturing Centre in Papuan Prehistory: The Causes and Implications. *Mankind* 11(3): 406-15.

MALINOWSKI, B. 1915. The natives of Mailu; preliminary results of the Robert Mond Research work in British New Guinea. *Transactions of the Royal Society of South Australia* 39: 494-706.

NEWTON, D. 1961. *Art Styles of the Papuan Gulf.* New York, The Museum of Primitive Art.

ORAM, N.D. 1968. Culture Change, Economic Development and Migration among the Hula. *Oceania* 38(4): 243-75.

THE PAPUA NEW GUINEA PLACE NAMES COMMITTEE. 1974. *Papua New Guinea Gazetteer.* Port Moresby, The Papuan New Guinea Place Names Committee.

PURSE, B. 1980. Camera on Expedition. *Australian Natural History* 20(1): 13-14, 19-22.

SAVILLE, W.J.V. 1926. *In Unknown New Guinea.* London, Seeley Service and Co.

SELIGMANN, C.G. 1910. *The Melanesians of British New Guinea.* Cambridge, The University Press.

SINCLAIR, J. 1978. *Wings of Gold: How the Aeroplane Developed New Guinea.* Sydney, Pacific Publications.

SOUTER, G. 1963. *New Guinea: The Last Unknown.* Sydney, Angus and Robertson.

STEPHENS, M.E. 1974. *With Bar Sinister on his Chicken Feathers: A Study of the Integration of Kin Terminology with Social Structure in Wanigela, Northern District, Papua New Guinea.* Unpublished Ph.D., University of North Carolina, Chapel Hill.

VANDERWAL, R. 1983. Kinomere Village, Papua: Sixty Years after Hurley. Paper presented to the National Conference of the Museums Association of Australia, 15-18 October, 1983, Melbourne.

WILLIAMS, F.E. 1923a. *The Collection of Curios and the Preservation of Native Culture.* Territory of Papua Anthropological Report No. 3.

WILLIAMS, F.E. 1923b. *The Vailala Madness and the Destruction of Native Ceremonies in the Gulf Division.* Territory of Papua Anthropological Report No. 4.

WILLIAMS, F.E. 1924. *The Natives of the Purari Delta.* Territory of Papua Anthropological Report No.5.

WILLIAMS, F.E. 1930. *Orokaiva Society.* London, Oxford University Press.